The *A*theist Camel
Rants Again!

ISBN: 1460933915
EAN13: 9781460933916
Library of Congress Control Number: 2011902801

Cover concept by Susanna Sharp-Schwacke

The *A*theist Camel Rants Again!

More arguments and observations from the atheist front

Bart Centre
as Dromedary Hump

Dedicated to atheist activists and freethinkers
past and present who have paved the way
for freedom of thought.

*"I will not attack your doctrines nor your creeds if they
accord liberty to me. If they hold thought to be dangerous—
if they aver that doubt is a crime, then I attack them one
and all, because they enslave the minds of men."*

—Robert G. Ingersoll, *The Ghosts*

Contents

Introduction

The visibility and influence of religion on the cultural front hasn't much diminished since the publication of my last book, *The Atheist Camel Chronicles*. Evangelical preachers continue to make proclamations that attribute deaths from natural disaster and war to their God's disappointment with man's lack of morality and impenitence. A conservative pope continues to dip his fingers in the blood of millions as he ignores science and condemns condom use.

The clergy remains in the headlines as new evidence of Church complicity in ministerial child molestations is unearthed. Theistically inspired school board activists continue to distort history and proffer pseudo-science to promote their religio-political agenda. Jihadists, both Muslim and Christian, continue to demonstrate, rage, burn, threaten, and kill in the name of their deity and prophet. Given these realities, it is disheartening and difficult to see any light for civilization at the end of a dark religious tunnel.

But advancement is not always the product of cataclysmic events. Much like evolution, it often comes in slow, subtle, incremental changes. Organizations such as the Freedom from Religion Foundation, Americans United for the Separation of Church and State, and the Military Religious Freedom Foundation have scored many significant wins against creeping theocracy and religious oppression in the US. More wins than losses— wins that help establish precedence for reason over religion. We owe the leadership and membership of these watchdog protectors of our rights and defenders of the Wall of Separation a great debt. That debt is best repaid by joining and supporting their tireless efforts.

On a smaller scale, but just as importantly, free-thinking authors, bloggers, local and college humanist and atheist groups, and individual atheists continue to raise awareness, shake apathy, and inspire activism. Even those who must suppress their acceptance of reason over myth and keep it hidden lest it impair relations with family, friends, or co-workers serve the cause. By strengthening the foundation of their rationality through readings, by subtly questioning and challenging theist "Truths," and by encouraging the next generation toward self-reliance and independent thinking...they also serve. I salute them and commend them for their courage.

Throughout this book you will find that I use the term "fundie" and "fundies." For the uninitiated, it is a shortened version of "fundamentalist." These are Christians (and, where applicable, also followers of other religions) who view their scripture as inerrant, infallible, written by God or with his divine inspiration; their belief in Creation, all the stories of the Bible, and all its miracles are taken as fact, not parable. The abbreviated term "fundie" is not used as an epithet in my writings, just a convenient abbreviated descriptor. I use other terms that cannot be mistaken for anything other than epithets.

Similarly, I use of the term "Xtian" and "Xtianity" randomly throughout the text as an abbreviation of "Christian" and "Christianity." This tends to enflame fundies as being disrespectful. Unfortunately, it isn't disrespectful albeit I have no particular reason to show respect for Christianity. The term "Xtian" is actually ancient and goes back to the Greek letter "chi" being used by the early Greek Christians as an abbreviation for "Christ." The symbol for the letter "chi" is "X."

Finally, this book is not written for believers unless they are on the fence, dangling their feet onto the side of rational thinking. If these essays help ignite their boldness and give them a push, excellent. It is not intended to try to win the minds of hardcore religionists to reality. While I may toy with and engage them on the net, I have long ago come to realize that proselytizing to those to whom reason is the enemy and to be avoided at all costs is a waste of my time. Thus, to those who question how I could possibly expect to break through to religionist minds and win them over to reason with my unrepentant, sometimes mocking, and unapologetic style, the answer is plain: I don't.

If these essays can assist freethinkers in debate, challenge thought, raise awareness, prompt more activism, provide some modicum of wisdom and guidance in a religionist majority society, or just make them laugh, this offering's objective will have been achieved.

Bart Centre
AKA, Dromedary Hump

1

"Atheism = Communism = Immorality": The Mantra of the Theistically Confused

24 Mar 2009

The theist propensity to equate Communism with atheism and vice versa is a function of two things: basic lack of understanding of what Communism is and what atheism isn't.

Joseph Stalin killed millions. A psychopath and paranoid, he embodied the strong-man, iron-fisted methods used by tyrants to retain power since time immemorial. One need only think of the biblical story of the pharaoh killing all first-born Hebrews to understand. The pharaoh didn't kill them because he was a pagan, or even because they were Hebrews. He acted to prevent a prophesized leader from emerging who would free the Hebrews, to ensure his power base and the Hebrews' continued enslavement—a simple question of economics. How do we know this? Because had his mythical actions been intended to eradicate the Hebrews, he wouldn't have stopped with just killing the first-born.

It wasn't an issue of pagan immorality vs. monotheistic morality—it was a political imperative. How different that is from the Hebrew God's commandment to eradicate all pagan tribes in their territorial path: men, women (except the virgins), children, and livestock.

While Communism embraces atheism, it does so in order to establish the State as the sole authority. It's a quasi-religion with the tyrant as its primate. It also recognized that the Church had a cohesive effect on the peasantry, and thus represented a potential threat to the State's exclusive power. Stalin never killed in the name of "godlessness"; he killed in the name of retention of one-man rule and the omnipotent power of the State.

"Uncle Joe" didn't just single out the religious for his murderous purges. He feared intellectuals, homosexuals, and anyone with a political perspective different from his own, including differing interpretations of Communism (note the similarity to the Church's targets of persecution for centuries: other religions, Protestant sects, and upstart cults like the Cathars). He had Trotsky removed and ultimately killed, along with untold thousands of other potential rivals and challengers.

Was this because of his lack of belief in God/gods? Was his rallying cry to his faithful followers, "Kill the theists in the name of atheism"? Hardly. Theists weren't even the primary concern. One may as well blame Stalin's education in a seminary for his genocidal acts.

Theists will oft regroup and say: *"Okay, fine, but Stalin and Mao represent a lack of morality and ethics that results from the rejection of God and God's laws."* But morality and ethics predate Christianity and monotheism. The ancient Egyptians, Greeks, Chinese, and Persians had laws and a code of ethics and morality, as did every highly developed or developing civilization. And yet this scope of genocidal destruction by a king of his own people was unknown in pagan pre-Judeo-Christian times. Additionally, and more currently, most people are familiar with the US Bureau of Prisons report that shows the rate of criminality is much higher among believers than non-believers, which, among other evidence, renders the claim of atheists' lack of ethics and morality debunked.

Atheism is defined as having no belief in God or gods. That's all. There is no hierarchy, no belief system. Communism, like religion, has a hierarchy; it is an entire belief system with a focal point of worship (the State), a dogma, doctrine, and expectation of compliance to that doctrine with a threat of punishment for noncompliance. In that regard, Communism has much more in common with religion than it does with atheism.

To attribute Joseph Stalin's or Mao's psychopathic tyrannical actions to their atheism, as opposed to their mental illness, hunger for power, and fanatical devotion to their political belief system, is tantamount to attributing Edward I's ("Longshanks") murderous suppression of the Scots and Welsh to his theism (when only his persecution of English Jews can be attributed to his Christian beliefs).

This distinction and the logic it represents are largely lost on or, more precisely, ignored by religionists. After years of indoctrination that Communism=Atheism=Lack of Morality, it's an uphill battle to get them to admit the fallacy. But then understanding the facts, like understanding evolutionary theory, wouldn't help their cause, so why should they?

Additionally, recognition of this reality wouldn't give theists a counter-argument for the millions of deaths attributable directly to religious fervor—killing for Yahweh or for Christ, executions of heretics, witches, et al.

No, they have no impetus to understand or reject their hackneyed Communism/atheist/morality confusion and delusion. So their self-imposed confusion marches on.

2

The "Religion Section"
Gets Proper Placement

21 Apr 2009

I noticed something interesting in my local newspaper the other day. After reading the main news and business sections, next was the religion section. It's a weekly part of the paper. It's not a very large part—one folded page/four printed sides. But, interestingly, only one and a half of those pages are actually devoted to religion. This is, after all, New Hampshire, where religion takes a backseat to living, logic, and lobster.

There's typically one religion story on the lead page. I always peruse it since one never knows if there will be some good fodder for my blog, or something to animate me to write a scathing letter to the editor debunking some theist's crazy statement. This week's story was devoted to Catholicism. Boring. I turned the page and browsed the announcements that take up half of page two: all-you-can-eat church buffets, church bingo events, church tag sales, church raffles, church pancake breakfasts, priest singles night, an alter boy molestation seminar, and previews of the coming Sunday's sermons from churches all over the area.

Then what I noticed for the first time about the "religion section" made me laugh out loud. On the bottom half of page two was "Strange News Stories" from around the country; you know the type: *"Dumb Crook Holds Up Bank with Skunk," "Deer Locked in Baskin Robbins Store Gets Ice Cream Headache,"* etc., etc. On the third page of the religion section were the comics, the horoscope, and Ann Landers' advice column. Page four was a full-page business ad.

The comics, daily horoscope, funny news from around the country, and an advice column for the chronically befuddled all grouped together there in the religion section!!

It caused me to ponder...do they group all the laughable, superstitious, and patently useless parts of the paper together in the religion section on purpose, or is this just a coincidence? I'm thinking the former. Either way, it couldn't be more appropriate. No sense mixing important real world events, information, and fact with superstition, humor, pseudo-science, and advice to the confused and weak-minded.

I wonder if this is a common practice or peculiar to New Hampshire. Check out your paper; you may be living in a less religiously infected area than you think. Or maybe your newspaper's publisher is an atheist.

3

Your Bling Belongs to Jesus

25 Apr 2009

A devout Xtian woman attempted to explain to me that all possessions/material things are owned by God/Jesus, that she/we are only using them like some kind of a lend lease program. There is nothing in the New Testament to support such a whacky notion. But in the Hebrew Bible, there are some verses that lead these folks to this conclusion. Here are some examples:

Deut. 10:14 "...the heaven of heavens is the LORD's thy God, the earth also, with all that therein is."

Psalm 50:12 "If I were hungry I would not tell you, For the world is Mine, and all it contains."

Job 41:11 "Who has given to Me that I should repay him? Whatever is under the whole heaven is Mine."

Haggai 2:8 "'The silver is Mine and the gold is Mine, declares the LORD of hosts."

So, if taken and applied literally, private property doesn't exist. But there's a problem. Since the Talmud has very specific guidelines for what one does to a thief, how is this reconciled with property not being owned by the individual but by God? Presumably the plaintiff would have no standing in court since the stolen items wouldn't be owned by him. Only God could sue/seek recompense. But God wouldn't sue; since the goods have simply changed hands to another "user," no damage has been done. It's a victimless crime. It was God's will.

And how does this jibe with Jesus saying: *"Render unto Caesar the things which are Caesar's, and unto God the things that are God's"* (Matthew 22:21)?

Clearly the coin of the realm is material wealth that Jesus had no interest in nor claim on.

And then there is this contradiction: *"The heaven, even the heavens, are the LORD's: but the earth hath he given to the children of men"* (Psalm 115:16).

Oops!

And this verse that credits not God but Satan with owning everything on earth:

"The devil taketh him up into an exceeding high mountain, and sheweth him all the kingdoms of the world, and the glory of them; And saith unto him, All these things will I give thee" (Mathew 4:8-9).

So what's going on here? That God/Jesus owns everything is clearly a faulty concept, a misinterpretation of scripture, and is rife with multiple contradictions. Further, to imbue a god with ownership of what one earns, buys, and accumulates in a material world is to attribute to a spirit being some vested interest in worldly goods. But some theists are so devoid of self-respect, self-reliance, and self-esteem, and are so dependent on their imaginary friend, they can't conceive of being worthy to own anything free and clear on their own...thus it must be God's!

Why would Jesus want to claim ownership of that Xtian's mobile home full of cats and old *TV Guides*? And if her car isn't hers, how come she keeps hiding it from the repo man? Questions to ponder.

4

Swine Flu End-Times Fulfillment

29 Apr 2009

Well, seems ole Jesus is playing with pigs one more time. No, he's not infecting pigs with demons (Mark 5); this time he's infecting humans with pigs' virus. What a character.

It didn't take long for the Christian soothsayers to start crediting Jesus with the swine flu outbreak. That's right—I said "crediting" because this is a good thing to them. Here's an example of a self-appointed prophet of God issuing his advance notice that this is the big one, the precursor to the End Times, the Rapture, Christ's return, HALLELUJAH!!! http://jgrantswankjr.blogspot.com/2009/04/swine-flu-prophecy-plagues-of-end-times.html

The key to his crazed ranting is this passage: Mathew 24:7—*"For nation shall rise against nation, and kingdom against kingdom: and there shall be famines, and pestilences, and earthquakes, in divers places."*

Can it be any more obvious? Between wars in Iraq and Afghanistan, unrest between Iran and the US,

Korea and the US, Venezuela and the US, famine in Africa, the massive earthquake in Italy, and now the swine flu pestilence, it's as obvious as the Virgin Mary's intact hymen that it's all about to hit the fan for us non-believers, while a free ride to Candy Land is in store for the faithful. The prophesy is about to be fulfilled. Thank ya, Jeezus!

Oh, sure, there are also conspiracy theorists on the net proclaiming swine flu is a terrorist attack, or a New World Order covert attempt to reduce world population. But no one is really going to buy those crazies, not when the Bible itself so plainly spells out the signs that announce Jesus is about to come down and open up a can of whoop-ass on the godless heretics. Besides, internet Christian prophets are all abuzz, and they can't *all* be wrong...can they?

So here's the plan. Put on a big gold cross, maybe burn all your heretical books and CDs on your front lawn, and squeal your everlasting devotion to Jesus, the Lord of the Pigs. Oink loud and maybe writhe around on the ground like the really hardcore True Christians do. You may still catch the swine flu, but at least if you expire you'll be assured of eventual resurrection with the rest of the believers who died in all the other pandemics.

I'm guessing a major pork product BBQ in paradise is being prepared. Bring your own Wet Ones.

5

Gay Marriage and Imported Religious Ire Coming to a State Near You

20 May 2009

Last week, the New Hampshire State Senate approved by a narrow margin a bill that would permit homosexual marriage, following Massachusetts' and Vermont's lead. Our governor, a moderate Democrat, has said he believes marriage should be strictly between a man and a woman, but has not decided if he would veto the bill or sign it.

Mrs. Hump and I wrote Governor Lynch to express our support for the law. We reminded him that ten years from now, when gay marriage is the norm across the country, his opposition to the law would be analogous to the religious fanatics and hate-mongers who opposed inter-racial marriage and made it illegal in some states not so very long ago—politicians who today are roundly deplored and held up as examples of the worst kind of Americans. I'm betting he'll sign the law.

What prompted us to write the governor was a story in *The Baptist Press* that called upon the faithful from across the country to phone the NH governor's office encouraging him to veto the law. I hate it when religious nuts from outside New Hampshire meddle in our affairs. The whole story can be found here: http://www.bpnews.net/BPnews.asp?ID=30411.

Naturally, they invoked scripture as their justification for opposition while pledging they held no homophobic or intolerant feelings toward gays (as though there is some difference between their religion's support of homophobia and subjugation of human rights, and their own intolerant behavior). Churches across the country are in a veritable frenzy over New England's shift toward gay marriage acceptance.

So, along with emailing the governor's office, I dropped the good Xtians at *The Baptist Press* a thank-you note. Here it is:

Dear Baptist Press,

If we hadn't read your story, my wife and I wouldn't have realized there was an organized attempt by people outside of New Hampshire to try to influence our governor to veto the Gay Marriage Bill. Now that we know this, we have been moved to contact Gov. Lynch and implore him to support equal rights and recognition of all humans and sign the bill.

It wasn't long ago that religious fanatics and racist government officials forbade inter-racial marriage. Most of us look back on those days as an embarrassment, indicative of the worst kind of ignorance and hate. The scripture was misused back then too, to support those hateful laws.

It doesn't surprise us that Baptists were at the forefront of that effort as well. Religious fanaticism often breeds hate, intolerance, and false claims of higher morality. The first president of the South Carolina Baptist Convention, Furman, proved that when he invoked scripture to justify slavery in the nineteenth century. I'm sure you are proud.

Our guess is life will go on long after homosexuals marry, and religionists have been reduced to the irrelevance they so justly deserve.

Feel free to use this letter as reference for future use because full rights of citizenship will be coming to your state soon, and so will the out-of-state religious homophobes.

6

In Defense of a Christian Bigot

08 May 2009

In the wake of the Miss America contest, the Internet and the media have been roundly piling on evangelical Xtian and homophobe par excellence, Miss California. It's a veritable feeding frenzy. I have two positions that may appear at odds with each other:

1. Miss California's position disgusts me.
2. She is being unfairly crucified.

"What's this?" you say. *"Hump defending a fanatical religionist homophobic twit? How is this possible?"* Well, it comes down to a matter of fairness.

Let's be realistic—this was a beauty pageant. Its only raison d'être is to feed men's and Rosie O'Donnell's masturbatory fantasies. The kinds of questions they have typically asked these silicon-enhanced Barbie dolls usually revolve around world peace, world hunger, saving children, or what their favorite color is. Instead, Miss California was presented with a stacked deck.

She never should have been asked that question on gay marriage. It was asked by a homosexual judge who had an axe to grind and very likely knew her position before he asked it. Even if he didn't, the fact that he asked it and got an answer he didn't like, and that is counter to what most enlightened people believe, is no grounds for her demonization.

If she hadn't clearly been lambasted and piled on for her conservative perspective, honestly answered, then it's likely she would have won the pageant, and never would have taken to the anti-gay/religious testimony campaign trail that she's on. The monster that created her post-pageant activism was a pageant official with an agenda, and political correctness run amok. The fact that four- or five-year-old nude pictures were suddenly dredged up appears as just another attempt to get back at her for her anti-gay position.

Let's look at this another way: if a candidate were asked about her "spiritual" perspective, and she answered she was an atheist and rejects the concept of spiritualism, where do you think that would lead? And after she was discarded as an unacceptable Miss America, if she went on the campaign trail and aired her opposition to religion and its hypocrisy, how many Christian blogs, organizations, and media sources would be pointing fingers and saying, "*See? She's a hater, just like all atheists. She didn't deserve to win. Let's go find more dirt with which to discredit her.*"

If a contestant is asked a question that has two possible answers, and one of those answers will cause her to be negatively viewed/demonized/disqualified, even though it's answered truthfully, then that question is not a valid challenge to her mental acuity or depth… it's a set-up.

It's tantamount to the "God gives free will" nonsense that Christians argue: "*Sure,*" they say, "*you have free will to believe in God or not, but if you decide NOT, then you burn in hell for eternity.*" What kind of "free will" option is that?

Let's be clear: I have no sympathy for her religious idiocy, and the stunted troglodyte-like social position it precipitates. But I know a lynching when I see one. I, for one, won't participate in it. To do so would be too Christian.

7

The Holy Foreskin Obsession

11 May 2009

It seems that Jesus' foreskin holds a revered place in Christian lore. Who'd have guessed that a religion whose followers are so…uh…"flaccid" when it comes to their icon's Judaic roots and practices would have such a fixation? But for over fourteen hundred years there has been a rather unhealthy affinity for Jesus' penis tip. Call it "holy penis envy."

On January first each year, Lutherans, Anglicans, and Eastern Orthodox Catholics observe the holiday called *"Circumcision of Christ."* This holy day marks Jesus' submission to Judaic law and tradition. In accordance with Jewish law, Jesus was circumcised on the eighth day after his birth. The Catholic Church decided back in 1969 to quit observing the fourteen-century-old holy day of the *"Feast of Circumcision"* (appetizing), and instead decided to rename it *"Solemnity of Mary, Mother of God"* day. Small wonder, given the former feast's implied menu.

If that weren't bizarre enough, there have been at least twelve official and unofficial Jesus foreskin relics revered and passed along among churches, popes, and devout nobles throughout Europe from the ninth through the sixteenth century. These were the Holy Prepuces. They kept them in special jeweled boxes, "whipping them out" only for very special occasions and celebrations...each church and owner attesting that only their prepuce was the one true foreskin of their Lord and Savior. Think I'm making this up? Here's a "tip" for you: Google "Holy Prepuce."

In fact, medieval paintings depicting the circumcision of Jesus were a hot commodity in the good old days.

Well, things got so out of hand, what with all of this unseemly Jesus penis talk, that in 1900 the Catholic Church threatened excommunication for any "putz" daring to write or talk about Jesus' holy member. The penalty became "stiffer" in 1954, when violation of the rule earned the highest level of excommunication, which included being shunned.

Unfortunately, during the Reformation and French Revolution, almost all of these penis pieces were destroyed or lost. Only one remained into the twentieth century, The Holy Prepuce of Calcata, which was "exposed," put on display, and taken for a walk through the streets of that Italian city annually as recently as 1983. The yearly practice would probably still be going on today had they not been "shafted" by some thief who stole it, jeweled box and all. What a "dick"!

So, why this Christian "hard-on" for Jesus' foreskin? Hey, who knows what makes Christian cultists tick. Headhunters have their shrunken heads, voodoo practitioners have their dried bats and such, and Christians favor their man-god's manhood. I guess one could say all other religions' relics just don't "measure up."

As a non-believer, I tried to equate this to some peculiar secular practice. But I never heard of anyone claiming to own Woody Allen's, Sigmund Freud's, or Isaac Asimov's excess penis part. For some reason, freethinkers just aren't "hung" up on the attraction. Maybe it's because we aren't "schmucks."

"Christianity Will Outlive Everything"

19 May 2009

I consider myself something of a connoisseur of platitudinous fundie statements—the crazier the better. It takes a sharp eye and an appreciation for the absurd to spot and savor some of the most bizarre things fundies say while in the throes of religious fervor. They rarely consider whether or not it makes sense, but they take great pride in proffering a statement that emphasizes their level of devotion to their religious infirmity.

A couple of weeks ago, in response to an article in which Karl Rove was bemoaning Christianity's eventual demise in a secular world, "Matthew," the Xtian in question, was moved to make this insightful comment:

"And on the subject of Christianity going away: The Constitution will pass away, the United States of America will pass away, everything will pass away but Christianity will endure forever."

That statement demonstrates the patented vacant thinking of the Xtian fundie. If *"everything,"* thus all life, passes away while Christianity endures, exactly

who or what is left to observe the belief system and rituals of Christianity? How will the faith be maintained?
How can a belief system continue/be propagated when
no adherents exist to believe in it?

Given that he probably never thought about this (in-
depth thinking not being a valued attribute amongst
these folks), once faced with this problem, Matt would
probably introduce something like: *"The angels will still
be Christians,"* or *"Jesus, God, and the Holy Spirit will be
Christians…and they live forever, as do the angels and all
dead believers' spirits."* After all, when you're invested in
superstition, why not invoke angels, deities, and dead
things to carry on the faith? It's not like he isn't already
fully invested in supernatural nonsense and might
damage his credibility.

My theory on how Christianity could outlive mankind is much simpler: cockroaches! Yes, cockroaches
will become the replacement Christians. Cockroaches
have survived millions of years, weathering all the cataclysmic geologic, atmospheric, and climatic events.
Surely they will outlive man and adopt Christianity
as their belief system. Picture it: praying cockroaches,
cockroach televangelists, cockroach faith healers,
cockroaches talking in tongues, cockroaches denying
science, cockroach priests, and cockroach ministers
molesting juvenile cockroach believers.

On further consideration, perhaps not. Christianity is doomed to extinction, just as all religions eventually succumb. Cockroaches are too smart to be suck-
ered into all that foolishness.

9

What Kind of God Punishes Knowledge? Guess Who

28 May 2009

In Greek mythology, Prometheus gave fire, which he stole from Zeus, to mortals. Zeus punished him by having him chained to a rock where every day a bird of prey ate out his liver, only to be regenerated daily in perpetuity .

Also in Greek myth, Arachus was a mortal who challenged the goddess Athena to a weaving contest. She lost, and Athena turned her into the first spider for her hubris.

Artemis was the virgin goddess of the moon and hunting. A mortal named Actaeon was out hunting when he came upon Artemis bathing in a stream and stopped to look. For his peeping tom-ism, Artemis had him turned into a deer, and he was promptly torn to pieces by his own hunting dogs.

These kinds of stories abound in ancient myths from many cultures. Man insults, challenges, or steals from the gods, and a swift and hideous punishment follows. But the theme of an angry and punishing god isn't just a pagan one. The God of Abraham, the Judeo-Christian God, was no slouch when it came to meting out punishment. And, yet, there is something very different about what this God punishes.

The very first punishment God hands out is to Adam and Eve. What dastardly deed did they do to deserve being banished from paradise, cursed with toil, pain, disease, the loss of immortality, and having the same punishment handed down to their children and all subsequent generations? Did they conspire to see God naked? Did they steal a sacred element? Did they challenge God's omnipotent ability?

No. Their unforgivable crime was they dared to eat from the Tree of Knowledge. That is, they dared to taste logic, reality, and fact. Imbibing in knowledge is a no-no. Knowledge is bad. Ignorance, mindlessness, drone-like stupidity is God's preferred state for his creations.

Why? Why was knowledge so guarded, so valued by this God, or, more specifically, by the writers of the Old Testament, that for man to desire it, achieve it, possess it is a cause for horrific punishment for all generations? Because with knowledge comes reasoning. With reasoning comes questioning and understanding. With understanding comes challenge to authority. Whose authority? The priestly class' authority.

The moral of the story the Old Testament writers wanted to get across loud and clear was simple: knowledge is not to be desired or achieved; it is a thing of danger in the wrong hands. For mortal men to pursue it can only lead to trouble. After all, look what it did to Mankind thanks to Adam and Eve. *"So shut the hell up and do as we tell you, 'cause that's all you need to know!!"*

And so it continues, taken to extremes by the early Church and practiced right into the twenty-first century by fundie Christians: the self-imposed ignorance, the blind, unquestioning compliance to ancient dogma, the disdain for and opposition to science and secular learning. Knowledge is to be avoided, for it is the enemy of the Church, or, as Martin Luther said: *"Reason is the Enemy of faith."*

Attaining knowledge is worse than stealing from the gods, or trying to see them naked. Knowledge = punishment; ignorance = bliss and reward. One needs to be a believer not to see the obscenity of such a doctrine.

10

Have We Had Enough of Their "Christian Love" Yet?

01 Jun 2009

Yesterday, a respected OBGYN was murdered by an anti-abortionist religious fanatic demonstrating that famous Christian love. Dr. Tiller was in his Kansas church, volunteering as an usher, when he was killed.

While the act is being publicly condemned by religious anti-abortion organizations whose history is rife with incitement to kill abortion providers, secretly they revel in the news. Indeed, there are postings all over the Internet by good, loving Christians openly applauding the murder and wishing he'd died a more horrible and slow death.

No doubt there will be those self-appointed arbiters of who is and isn't a Christian who will pronounce the murderer and those who celebrate his act as "not *true* Christians." How very convenient, how predictable, how self-serving.

Hardly a day goes by when the media doesn't report a minister, priest, deacon, Christian youth counselor, etc. molesting a child here or abroad and the Church covering it up or downplaying it.

Hardly a month passes when we don't hear of a Christian parent letting their child die of a treatable disease, or evading court order for treatment, because they preferred to trust in God to heal the child.

Hardly a week expires when we don't read of anti-Semitic scrawling on synagogues, or the destruction of Jewish cemeteries somewhere in this country or Europe; or evangelical soldiers and chaplains aggressively proselytizing Muslims in war zones against standing orders, or harassing and threatening non-Christian servicemen in their proselytizing zeal.

Then there's the anti-gay marriage crusade of those loving Christian activists whose lives and freedoms and marriages are somehow mysteriously and inexplicably diminished by the state's recognition of the union of two loving humans with matching genitalia.

And who can forget the inspiring words of the pope, who, barely two months ago, against all medical scientific reality, blamed the use of condoms for spreading the AIDS virus in Africa, using his influence among the ignorant to further the spread of the disease in the most devastated continent on the planet?

Didn't we have enough of their infamous "Christian love" during the Dark Ages, the Middle Ages, and the Inquisition to last us forever? Evidently not. The love goes on. Dog save us.

11

Eating God's Body: Has Christianity *Any* Originality?

11 Jun 2009

Here's a quiz: what tastes like a stale piece of matzo and cheap wine?

If you answered "a dead Jewish man-god," you're partially right.

In 1 Corinthians 11:23-25, Paul says:

"For I have received of the Lord that which also I delivered unto you, That the Lord Jesus the same night in which he was betrayed took bread: And when he had given thanks, he brake it, and said, **Take, eat: this is my body,** *which is broken for you: this do in remembrance of me. After the same manner also he took the cup, when he had supped, saying,* **This cup is the new testament in my blood: this do ye, as oft as ye drink it,** *in remembrance of me."*

Christians refer to this practice as the consumption of the Eucharist. Jesus, what an original guy. Leave it to him to come up with this unique and singularly Christian way of remembering and internalizing himself as one's special friend.

Whoa, not so fast! It seems Jesus, or, more precisely, the writers of the Jesus myth borrowed this delightful practice of symbolic cannibalism from ancient pagan religions. The religious practice is called *theophagy*, literally "god-eating."

In the book *The Golden Bough* by Sir James G. Frazer, the many pagan religions that symbolically gobbled up their gods are covered in great detail. Particularly notable was the Greek god Dionysus, son of the supreme god, Zeus. Grain and wine were substitutes for his body and consumed by his worshipers as part of their religious rites.

Interestingly, Dionysus was the result of Zeus impregnating a human woman. Dionysus wandered Asia teaching people how to cultivate vineyards. There are other similarities between him and the Jesus story. Indeed, there are a number of scholars, among them Rudolph Bultman and, more recently, Barry B. Powell, who attribute Jesus' turning of water into wine to Dionysian legend (of particular interest, Bultman was Lutheran, a professor of theology, and a New Testament scholar).

That symbolic ingestion of one's favored god was incorporated into Christianity along with so many other pagan practices (i.e., All Saints Day/Celtic Halloween, Easter/celebration of the Spring equinox, Christmas/celebration of the winter solstice, the concept of Trinity/Hinduism, etc.) shouldn't be much of a surprise to anyone except to Christians, to whom knowledge of such things is best left unlearned.

Jesus cookie with a sip of Chianti—a meal fit for the worshipers of a pagan man-god, or a very unoriginal king of the Jews.

12

What's More Christian Than Praying for the Death of the President?

16 Jun 2009

"*Imprecatory Psalms [are those prayers]...which invoke judgment, calamity, or <u>curses</u>, upon one's enemies or those perceived as the enemies of God. ... As a sample...Psalm 139:9 which declares 'Happy shall he be, that taketh and dasheth thy little ones against the stones...'*"
http://en.wikipedia.org/wiki/Imprecatory_Psalms

Christian apologetics' websites allot thousands of words to the subject of imprecatory prayer. Mostly they are convoluted, double-talking contradictions that simultaneously claim such prayers to be both righteous and wrong, justifiable and ill-advised, misinterpreted and clearly defined. Once again it seems their God hasn't made his meaning clear enough for them to get their opinions and acts together.

But the short story is that praying for the death of someone who is your perceived enemy or whom you have decided is the enemy of God is as Christian as can be. Fundies have no problem invoking God's help to kill people who are deemed their enemy.

An ex-Navy Christian chaplain prays for the death of Rev. Barry Lynn of Americans United for the Separation of Church and State, and Mikey Weinstein, the head of Military Religious Freedom Foundation. Why? What horrible things did these men do to justify calling upon God to smite them? Rev. Lynn is a leader in the effort to keep Church and State separate. And Mikey Weinstein fights to give servicemen the right to not be discriminated against for being other than Christian. Evidently that's a good reason to pray for their deaths. Here's the whole story: http://blog.au.org/2009/04/27/spiritual-warfare-exchaplain-prays-for-death-of-aus-lynn/

More recently, a former president of the Southern Baptist Christian Convention prays for the death of President Obama, and says it was prayers for Dr. Tillman's death that caused the assassination of the gynecologist and abortion provider. Further, he says that not employing imprecatory prayer to smite the godless is to fail as a Christian, for it is the duty of Christians to pray for the death of people whose ideas run counter to Christian beliefs. http://www.abpnews.com/index.php?option=com_content&task=view&id=4131&Itemid=53

Notice that they don't pray for these men to change their minds, to mend their wayward ways, or to come to Jesus...oh, no. Death prayers are the preferred appeal to God. Nothing says, "Let's fix this problem" like a heartfelt death prayer.

Praying for the death of law-abiding activist defenders of the Constitution, the president of the United States, and doctors who support women's right to choose are examples of that famous "Christian love" that is more than skin deep...it goes right down to the bone.

13

Blaming the Godless Messenger

20 Jun 2009

R ecently I was accused by a Christian friend of continuously focusing on media reports of the unseemly acts committed by Christians, both clergy and laypeople. You know: the murder of the abortion doctor, the acts of Fred Phelps, the molestation of kids by pastors, the torture of children by devout parents, etc.

Evidently, the fact that men of God and the gullible sheep they herd frequently commit atrocities and obscene acts of abuse and degradation toward their fellow man in the name of God/Jesus or to fend off Satan wasn't the primary concern. It's the *reporting* of it that irked him, as though I single-handedly might give religion a bad name, as though religion needs my assistance to accomplish that.

Invariably the old canard pops up: *"Anyone who calls themselves a Christian who perpetrates those acts is not a True Christian."* But this is nonsense. We have been alternately amused and disgusted by this tack for as long as certain Xtians and Christian fundamentalist sects have been holding themselves up as the arbiters of who is/isn't a Christian, in spite of what scripture and Jesus identified as prerequisites for being "saved"/ labeled Christian.

No, the condemnation, the complaint, this Christian has is with *me,* the messenger. Better these "fake" Christians' acts not be held up to scrutiny and dragged into the light of public opinion. Better the self-appointed arbiters of who is/isn't Christian be spared the embarrassment and indignity of having to explain away, apologize, or deny how a doctrine that claims a monopoly on morality and goodness breeds such disgusting behavior.

The media is full of these reports of theist atrocity. It's a weekly if not daily occurrence. A recent example is a forced exorcism on a child by his mother, who handcuffed him and denied him food for three days in order to purge "the demon" from his body. Here's the whole story: http://www.11alive.com/news/local/story. aspx?storyid=131511&catid=3.

Ask a Xtian: *"Without religion and its superstitions, from where would such a delusion leading to such abuse have originated?"* Their silence is deafening.

Whether it's hyper-religiosity caused by mental disease, or a minister taking advantage of a child by using his God-given authority to intimidate, these acts are there. They are real. They are committed by the devout the followers of a mythic man-god, the readers of and adherents to scripture. Often they justify the act in the name of scripture.

When the day arrives that an atheist tortures or murders his/her own child in the name of "NO God" or "NO Satanic possession," or a renowned atheist figure rapes a child and uses his atheism as leverage to get into that kid's pants and intimidate him into silence, I promise to report it. Until then, don't blame the godless messenger for the copious grotesque acts of the religiously infected. It comes with theist territory.

14

Deicide Is Dead! Long Live "Faithicide"

01 Jul 2009

Deicide–noun
1. a person who kills a god
2. the act of killing a god

I've occasionally pondered the word "deicide." It's a peculiar concept. Killing something that doesn't exist isn't a new idea, but from what I can ascertain it's the only act of fictional-character-killing that has its own word.

You never hear anyone accuse Dr. Abraham van Helsing, the protagonist of Bram Stoker's *Dracula*, of committing "Vampire-icide," nor is the word in the dictionary. Besides, how powerful can a god be if it can be killed by its own creations? There is nothing in scripture that indicates God is susceptible to kryptonite or the like.

No. The word makes zero sense. It should be dropped from the English lexicon, as *Webster's* did back in 1949 by deleting some words that were over two hundred years old and out of common usage. In its place

I recommend "faithicide," which connotes the erosion of theism by the advancement of science, reason, discovery, and intelligent discourse. It's not a new word. It has been used informally for a few years. But its time has come for formal recognition and common usage.

We are all complicit in "faithicide."

- Every time Dawkins, Hitchens, Harris, Dennette, Price, Ray, Ehrman, et al. publish one of their books, faith is being killed.
- Every time a freethinking organization posts an atheist display next to a Christmas display, and each time a bus rolls by with an anti-religion/pro-free thought message on its side, faith is being dissolved.
- Each time a secular watchdog organization challenges religious intrusions into our lives, faith is executed.
- Each time an atheist blog is posted, a debate initiated, or a religionist's letter to the editor is rebutted by a freethinker, faith is assassinated.
- With each new scientific discovery, faith is extinguished.

The erosion of theism in the modern world isn't happening by itself. It was cajoled, convinced, pushed, shoved, and forced kicking and screaming into its spiral of insignificance in the industrialized (read: educated) world. Faith's impotence as a means to an end, as a moral standard, as an explanation for the natural world has been exposed.

"Faithicide" deserves its place in our language and in our dictionaries. Definition: *killing religion with reason, one superstition at a time.*

Inevitably our practice of "faithicide" will succeed. There won't be any grand final deathblow; faith's ultimate demise will come slowly...a death of a thousand cuts of reason. When that happens, all that will remain to be done is to shovel dirt into the unholy grave of religiosity. Then, too, can *Webster* expunge "faithicide" from its pages.

15

Pity the Persecuted Christians

12 Jul 2009

"Here in America the persecution [sic] of Christians has not yet reached the feverish pitch as in other parts of the world. There is still a Constitution that protects them and allows them to freely practice their faith... Slowly, methodically, and incrementally the anti-God forces are working to remove that Constitutional barrier."

So reads an extract from a Christian website article called "War on Christianity." It goes on in great detail, decrying how prayer and the Bible have been removed from public school, how public property can't be used to display religious symbols, how churches are threatened with losing tax exemption for openly campaigning for a political candidate.

It claims unfair treatment by the media, bemoaning how religious events aren't given enough coverage on the major media outlets, and how religious leaders are intentionally cast as "cold and impersonal." Here's the site: http://www.jeremiahproject.com/prophecy/warxian.html.

They make it sound as though Christianity is undergoing a veritable Inquisition. Naturally, their perspective comes through the lens of people whose religious fervor infects every aspect of their life. They cannot differentiate between their right to practice their religion (which is never even implied) and the rights of non-Christians NOT to have the Christian religion forced upon them...which is precisely what they are protesting. By impeding their holy charge to proselytize, convert, harass, badger, and impose their beliefs on others, it is *they* who are being persecuted. That's about as bizarre a reversal of logic as one could conceive.

There are many other Christian sites that, in the best tradition of their whining martyrs and saints before them, claim persecution at the hands of "secular America."

The funny thing is that 78 percent of Americans are Christians. The vast majority of elected government officials are Christian. Seven of the nine Supreme Court justices are Christian (the other two are Jewish). But that doesn't seem to occur to them. Evidently the 16 percent of the country that comprises atheists and agnostics is united and powerful enough to conspire to bring about the demise of Christianity in America. Sounds like a cross between Joseph McCarthy's Red Scare propaganda and the vast Jewish conspiracy myth.

Frankly, I wish it were so. If only Christians could experience genuine persecution just long enough to give them a firsthand taste of the true horrors that Christians themselves perpetrated for ages on the Jews, Muslims, Cathars, Coptic Christians, "heretics,"

atheists, "witches," early scientists, homosexuals, various Christian sect offshoots, and indigenous peoples
who refused capitulation to Christianity.

Let the poor, put-upon US Christian majority experience the imprisonment, torture, pogroms, exiles,
discrimination, displacement, genocide, cultural
extinction, and exclusionism that their belief system
and religious fervor has perpetrated on people all over
the planet for almost two millennia. Then let them cry
that they are persecuted because they aren't allowed to
impose their hideous book of fables onto our children's
minds in public school. I weep for their downtrodden,
ghetto-confined, persecuted majority existence.

16

Conversation with a Devout Catholic Hairdresser

15 Jul 2009

I was getting my hair cut today in preparation for a book-signing on Sunday. The young lady, I'll call her Susie, has been cutting my hair for a few months now. She is attractive, friendly, gregarious, articulate, and normal in every way. I thought.

In casual conversation, I mentioned my book. She was stunned by the atheist theme, announced that she was a "devout Catholic," and told me lightheartedly that I'm going to Hell. "Hey, no problem here. I just hope Anne Frank knows how to play poker," I quipped. Blank stare from Susie. "Who's Anne Frank?" she asked.

Curious, I asked her exactly what she means by "devout Catholic"—how exactly does it differentiate her from "regular Catholic"? She replied, "Well, I go to mass every Sunday, don't practice birth control, oppose abortion for any reason, and am a conservative Republican." The last struck me as particularly weird since I don't recall anything in Catholic dogma that demanded a particular political position or specific party affiliation as a prerequisite for being Catholic, devout or otherwise. That Jesus was anything but conservative in his position on the ruling authority's practices and unforgiving scriptural interpretations hardly puts him the GOP's camp.

Being careful not to provoke anything that would cause her to carve a cross into the back of my head, I asked how often she read the Bible. She said she's never read it.

I asked: "Well, you believe in transubstantiation, I assume." She said she never heard that term, but she follows the teachings of Jesus. So I ask what teachings of Jesus in particular she admires. Susie's reply: "The Ten Commandments."

When I explain that the Ten Commandments preceded Jesus by fifteen-hundred years and were attributable to Moses, she said, "Oh, yeah, that's right. But Jesus followed the Ten Commandments because he was Jewish."

So I asked if she follows the same Jewish laws that Jesus did, as he told everyone they must: the ones in Leviticus, Deuteronomy, etc., like stoning unruly children to death, keeping kosher, not wearing mixed fiber clothes, not suffering witches to live...? "Some kids sure could use a stoning," she laughed. "But I don't believe in witches."

I could tell she had no idea what I was talking about. But then she volunteered that she'd rather die in childbirth and leave her other three kids, all under the age of nine, without a mother than terminate the pregnancy of a severely ill, malformed fetus that would likely not live more than a few hours. That was enough for me. There was a copy of a trashy celebrity magazine on her counter plastered with Michael Jackson's face (evidently he's still dead), which all of a sudden I found very interesting. I got a damn good haircut; I left her a 25 percent tip, set up the next appointment, and we said our goodbyes.

So, I had my answer. A devout Catholic is one who goes to church every week, has no concept of a foundational element of her religion (transubstantiation), doesn't practice birth control, never read the Bible, doesn't know who is credited with handing down the Ten Commandments, hasn't a clue what Jesus taught, is a conservative Republican, and would kill herself and leave her three children motherless to give a defective fetus an hour's worth of life.

Okay, got it. Thanks. Sorry I asked.

17

News Flash: "Great Debate" Finally Decides God Question!

20 Jul 2009

The following is taken directly from a Xtian's posting on an atheist board on July 18, 2009. Brace yourself for this shocking revelation:

A great debate between Dr. William Lane Craig (Christian) and Mr. Frank Zindler (atheist). After weighing the evidence from this great debate it is clear that it is time that you Atheists just accept that you are wrong. I am not here to debate you guys or stay in your little group. I will leave the debate up to the professionals in this great Debate that you all clearly need to watch :)

The polls from the great debate with two of the top debaters in their field results are listed below :)

- **7,778 people attended the debate with thousands & thousands more tuning in on TV and Radio Channels.**
- **6,168 filled out the ballots after the great debate**

- **97% voted the case presented for Chistianity** (sic) **was the most compelling by a long shot**
- **Even 82% of the non-christian** (sic) **voted the case presented for Christianity was stronger**
- **Even 47 people who came to the great debate indicated that they have now become believers**
- **Not one person became an Atheists** (sic)

Please Wake Up Now! Jesus Loves You :)
Jay Adams

Well, that settles that! Evidently this one and only *"great debate"* (as Jay proclaimed it approximately six times) was so lopsided, so overwhelming a victory for the supporters of God, that this jubilant believer accepts it as proof of God's existence and affirmation of his belief. He is so excited, so relieved, and so buoyed by the result that clearly he is ecstatic.

Indeed, how could we atheists all not just *"Wake up Now!,"* abandon all reason, and fall to our knees following said "great debate"? Plus, Jesus loves us! Sounds like a win-win for everyone, Jesus included.

Of course, the poor fellow had no idea this debate took place over eighteen months previous in January of 2008. And naturally Jay couldn't or wouldn't provide a source/link that substantiated those stats he provided because they were entirely made up by him or a Christian source he'd prefer not to divulge. After all, a little fabrication, embellishment, and hyperbole on behalf of the Lord has always been endorsed by the Christian fathers. As I've often said, lying is a sacrament to them. But, worse, they are such bad lies, so blatantly silly, that a child could see the fallacy of them, especially the conversion statements, irrespective of who presented the better argument.

After all:

- How could two men on a stage debating the existence/non-existence of the supernatural be perceived by any person with all their faculties as having proven, decided, and resolved an age-old issue to the point where anyone could proclaim the question settled once and for all?
- How does anyone listen to a single debate, discarding all previous debates and with no evidence or proof offered for the supernatural, and declare it a nullification of non-belief and validation of belief?
- Where would one find an audience of non-believers so devoid of thought that they'd "come to Jesus" and abandon their logic and reason simply as a result of the efficacy of one man's debate skills?
- How could the alleged "conversions" be verified as having been non-believers?

But most baffling of all, how does a Christian as insipid as Jay dress himself, find the bus stop, and get to his fry station at Burger King on time for the morning rush?

I wonder what it's like to be a fundie and never have to be burdened by genuine thought.

18

What's Behind Christian Inventiveness with Word Definitions?

24 Jul 2009

In *The Atheist Camel Chronicles*, I wrote a chapter on "Christian Speak," the translation into English of bizarre things Christians say. I also wrote one on how Christians try to give words in the Bible new meanings so as to better defend the absurd, contradictory, incongruent, and irrational words and actions of their God.

On a related note, and to round out the subject of Christians' propensity toward playing fast and loose with incongruent linguistics, I offer the following observation and analysis. I guess you could call it the third element in a trinity of Xtian religious language perversion.

A rather innocuous and inoffensive Christian fellow recently proffered that *"atheism is a religion."* That activist atheists/anti-theists such as myself, Dawkins, Hutchins, Harris, Meyers, et al, are *"the most religious"* people he knows. Evidently the basis for this is our outspoken opposition to religious delusion, our disdain for its negative effects on society, both historically and currently, and the agenda of some religionists to force their beliefs on others and intrude on our lives and freedoms. But to call atheism a religion or atheists religious is just moronic.

I tossed him the canard about how atheism is a religion like baldness is a hair color and how calling atheism a religion is to akin to calling *not* collecting stamps a hobby. As I feared, the analogies were lost on him.

I referred him to dictionary.com, suggesting he look up the definitions of "religion" and "atheism." By definition, atheism cannot be a religion. Any educated person who can read and has the desire to use language properly knows this. I also explained that if not believing in something is a religion then anyone who disbelieves in Bigfoot is part of the "non-belief in Bigfoot religion." (His will be done!) It went right over his head.

This theist is confusing a "position" with a religion. I have any number of positions on things. Here are a very few among hundreds, perhaps thousands, of positions I embrace:

- I tend toward liberal social politics, but moderate/conservative fiscal politics and I make that position known to my congressional representatives. (The religion of "Moderatism"?)
- I have a position on my right to own firearms, and am vocal on that as well. (The religion of "Pro-Gunism"?)
- I have a position on the stupidity of conspiracy theorists, and frequently write letters to the editor deriding and exposing their idiocy. (The religion of "Dismissal of Whacko-ism"?)

- I have a position on the non-existence of vampires, werewolves, faeries, fortune tellers, space alien visitors, etc., etc., albeit I don't feel the need to espouse it to most thinking people. (The religion of "Non-Boogie-Manism"?)
- I have a position on the use of camels for food. (The religion of "Non-Camel Cannibalism"?)

Unfortunately, there are a few atheists who, through their own stupidity, feed theist misconceptions of atheism. Some of them call for an "atheist church," or at least see no conflict with the oxymoronic term. These atheists are the Uncle Toms, the embarrassing mentally impaired relatives of the activist atheist movement who are best confined to an attic or their parents' basement.

So what causes this peculiar need for religionists to redefine words and stray so readily from their clearly defined meanings? Why can't they understand the simple concepts that have been codified in the English language for centuries without reprocessing them to fit their personal agenda? In a word: ignorance. It's their lack of thirst for knowledge, a disregard for learning, a limited intellect, and willingness to mouth the agenda-driven drivel of their apologists.

I'm not convinced religion causes believers this peculiar propensity toward perversion of definitions. I think the people who are attracted to religion are predisposed toward it and that their religious training and fervor, externally imposed or self-taught, simply reinforces it. That they are oblivious to it is just one more justification for my anti-religious position. I guess that makes me a congregant of the "First Church of Our Lady of No Patience for Vapidity."

19

Uncle Tom Atheists: Part of the Problem—No Part of the Solution

01 Aug 2009

Recently I came across something I've never previously experienced that stunned me. I touched on it briefly in my last essay but it deserves more exploration, or should I say exposure.

I'm talking about people who proclaim their atheism yet completely lack the will to break from their religious enslavement. As opposed to taking a stand, they are quick to acquiesce to theists, willing to appease them in order to not incur their wrath or rejection, and willing to attribute to religion a beneficence, beauty, and goodness (that they can neither name nor describe) in spite of their rejecting it themselves and in direct contradiction to reasoned analysis and historical evidence.

These are the atheists who give belief, any belief, their "respect." They see no threat from fundamentalists targeting the First Amendment's Establishment Clause for extinction. They turn a blind eye to

Creationist/ Intel Design attempts to dumb down curriculum and proselytize to our children in public schools. They have no problem, or if they do they dare not speak it, when Christian religious symbols and icons are placed on public property to the exclusion of all other religious and secular symbols. And, finally, among the worst of these are those who would attend an "atheist church" (whatever the hell that would be), or even a religious sect's house of worship in order to make theists "more comfortable" with them.

Maybe in my atheist activist vigilance, in my fight against fundamentalist extremism and intolerance, in my focus on preserving rights, my railing against the innumerable atrocities, injustices, and lies of the religious, I never gave much thought to the fact that there exists the ugly atheist relative in our midst.

These are the Uncle Tom atheists—the atheists who, comfortable in their anonymity and meekness of fortitude, happily cower in their non-confrontational apathy and shuck and jive in the presence of their theist "mas'as." They will openly condemn their activist atheist brethren for rocking the boat by calling extremist religionists what they are, thus "giving atheism a bad name," as if theists have always thought of us in only the kindest possible terms before. As if their demurring to the theist majority's demands and delusion and respecting their rejection of reality is to be praised and admired.

They will leave it to atheist activists past and present to fight blasphemy laws—activists who battled to ensure atheists have the right to hold public office when laws prevented it, who were scorned and shunned by their Christian neighbors for standing up for their rights, who stood before the Supreme Court and demanded that prayer not be imposed on children in public schools while Christians raged against them and threatened their lives. While the Neville Chamberlain-ish, religionist appeasing Toms condemn activist atheists as loud mouths and label our activism "counter-productive," they nonetheless are happy to reap the freedoms and benefits activists have secured for them.

No. I won't play the Christian game and declare these Uncle Tom atheists "not True atheists." By rejection of belief in God/gods they are as true an atheist as I am.

What I will say is this: I have more respect for Fred Phelps, who spews his hateful homophobic brand of Christian love, than I do for an Uncle Tom atheist. At least Fred has the passion of his convictions as perverse as they may be. Uncle Tom atheists are complacent, parasitic worms whose freedoms are nourished by the blood, sweat, and tears of the atheist activists they condemn. A pox on them.

20

Religion Is a "Beautiful Thing"

05 Aug 2009

❝ …I hear a lot of atheists who believe that religions are all wrong and must be killed off and what not. Even though I'm an atheist I think a religion can be a beautiful thing, in the hands of the right people.❞

I discovered this posting in an online message group. I was moved to respond as follows:

"Please, give me some examples of how religion is a *'beautiful thing in the hands of the right people.'*

"When you do that, please be sure to help me understand how the *beautiful thing* religion is could not be realized without the delusion of supernaturalism; the intolerance for others' non-belief or differing beliefs; the fiction of afterlife; the threat of eternal damnation and suffering; the cult-like worship of blood, pain and death; the rejection of scientific proofs and evidence; the enslavement of young minds to superstition and lies instead of reality, reason and knowledge; all of which are part and parcel to the theistic mindset.

"Are you saying that the beauty of religion lies in the charitable works of churches? If so, does that imply that charity is the sole provenance of religion? That good acts wouldn't exist without religion's promulgation of delusion and supernaturalism? That people of religion are driven to do altruistic things not because it is simply the humane and ethical thing to do, but because religion pressures, inspires, motivates them more so than the non-believers' altruistic instincts and actions? Or is it because religious charity is a way to proselytize to those desperately in need of material aid in an effort to gain converts? Is that the '*beauty of religion*'?

"Or perhaps its beauty lies in the fear religion seeks to instill in order to gain recruits and ensure compliance; the subservience to shaman-like authority; the false hope of life after death; the rejection of science and downplaying of secular knowledge?

"And who are these '*right people*' of whom you speak in whose hands this beauty is revealed? Mother Theresa? The pope? Phelps? Sharpton? Bakker, Falwel, Robertson, Wright, Graham, Huckabee, Brownbeck? The faith healers? The multi-millionaire televangelists? The terminally ill person who prays for pain relief or a cure that never comes? The crippled, deformed, and blind that flock to Lourdes in the hope of a restoration that never happens?

"Perhaps it's the proselytizing door-to-door missionary hucksters? The ministers/priests who molest and are protected by their church? The apologists who twist and turn scripture to make it appear to suit a kinder, gentler religion? The fundamentalist evolution deniers who want schools to teach myth as though it were science? The "Christian Nation" promoting radicals, who deny the facts of our nation's roots and our Founding Fathers' position on Christianity, distort history, and seek to tear down the 'wall of separation' between church and state?

"Were the Inquisitors the *'right people'*? The Crusaders? The witch burners? The anti-Semites and the religious leaders, like Martin Luther, who enflamed them? The suicide bombers? The book burners? The Christian Zionists, who want to see no peace in the Middle East, lest it impede the End-Times prophecy's fulfillment? The abortion-doctor killers? Those Christians who used the Bible to justify slavery, gender discrimination, and oppose inter-racial marriage?

"Maybe the *'right people'* are those faithful who pray over a sick child and watch them die when medical science could have restored them to health? Those who use scripture to justify subjugation of gays' rights, or the control of women's reproductive rights, or the military invasion of non-threatening nations? Those who conduct exorcisms on the weak or the mentally ill? The religionists who falsely claim condoms spread AIDS and thus condemn millions of third-world peoples to their death through unprotected sex? Those who justify killing for land ownership based on biblical precedence and divine will? Those who sacrifice their own lives to kill innocent 'infidels' to get their reward in paradise? Who indoctrinate their children to view non-followers as 'the other'? Who oppose women's rights because their scripture tells them women are less than men? Which of these are the *'right people'*? If none of them, then who?

"Religion is a mind virus, as Darrel Ray, the author of *The God Virus*, so eloquently proffers. That it has some connection with charitable works or because the false promise of life after death in Candy Land is comforting to those afflicted by religious fable, that its music, art, and architecture is often iconic, its rituals hypnotic in their pomp and spectacle, is hardly a validation of, or justification for, its deception, false promises, rejection of reason, exclusionism, and intolerance.

"Its '*beauty*' doesn't override the dependency, threats, fear, ignorance, hate, and misery it spreads through the brainwashing of the young, undereducated, desperate, and gullible. I see no beauty in deception. Show it to me.

"Yes, religion should be killed off. Fortunately, the scientific age and man's acceptance of reality is causing religion to self-destruct throughout the civilized world, none too soon and long overdue."

It has been three days and I'm still waiting for a response. I won't hold my breath, nor waste it on him any further.

21

The Proselytizing Playbook
10 Aug 2009

Here's the thing about religious fanatics who believe it is their duty to proselytize to the educated and uninfected: they haven't figured out yet that we have heard it all, read it all, rejected it all as fable.

They think by repeating their canned corn, their brainwashed dependency on ancient fable, their rejection of reality, distortions of fact, and reinterpretation of biblical scripture that suddenly every bit of knowledge we, the thinking, have accumulated through study, discourse, education, and investigation will suddenly be abandoned—dissolved like salt in so much water. It would be as though by quoting to them from the Egyptian Book of the Dead, we'd expect them to see the light and worship Isis or Ra.

I can't count how many times I've heard the same old pap that they draw from fundamentalist apologetics sites or JW pamphlets that have time and again been offered as some proof for supernaturalism. From great flood pseudo-science to Jesus' resurrection *"'cuz the Bible says so,"* to quoting John 3:16, to putting God's murderous rampages into a lovely light. Somehow all of this is supposed to get us to abandon what we know from science, natural law, history, our own reading of scripture and familiarity with comparative religions and pre-Abrahamic gods, and fall to our knees praising the Lard. You'd think by now they'd get the picture.

We've seen them all—argument by popular acceptance (*"How could so many people believe if it isn't true?"*), to grossly fallacious distortions of argument by authority (*"Einstein believed in a god"*), to the abandonment of fact and the craziest perversions of science (*"Scientists have proven the Ark exists/the great flood happened/that the earth is only six thousand years old"*), etc., etc. It's a veritable cornucopia of hackneyed, false, and vapid statements that anyone with a modicum of intellect and education can dispel with little effort.

So why does it persist? There are, in my experience, three causes for this irrational approach by the proselytizing fanatic:

1. They project on thinking people the same gullibility, lack of sophistication, stunted education, rejection of secular learning/history, lack of respect for fact, and disdain for evidence and the scientific method that they themselves embrace.

2. Since they believe their myth to be the only reality, they are incapable of seeing the correlation between all other man-made gods, and mythical figures and beings that carry exactly the same weight of evidence as does their preferred myth,

and which they readily reject because "those are fairy tales or false gods."

3. They are led to believe by their shamans and fundamentalist websites that atheists are just angry at God, or haven't heard the "good news" and all it takes is a little preaching to bring us into the fold. It's their duty and calling to inform us, as though it were possible for an educated adult in an industrialized country to have never heard about Jesus, to have never been exposed to Christian doctrine, one of the greatest travesties of the mind in two thousand years. And, here, some superstitious mind-slave is going to elucidate me.

There was a time when I enjoyed the opportunity to engage them and expose the foolishness of these apostles of magic, superstition, and stupidity. But as I get older, as I hear the same old hackneyed fluff offered as some new and revealed truth by the ignorant and deluded, my patience has worn thin. I become bored. A simple verbal bitch-slapping is all I have the time for.

22

Geocentrists Are the *True* Christians

15 Aug 2009

"*Modern geocentrism is the belief by extant groups that Earth is the center of the universe... This belief is often based on Biblical verses and is most common among American Protestants. This belief is directly opposed to scientific evidence that the Sun is essentially the gravitational center of the solar system, and that the location of the Earth is not privileged.*" http://en.wikipedia.org/wiki/Modern_geocentrism

As far back as 600 BCE, the Greek Ionians postulated that the Earth orbited the Sun, and that the Sun was the central point of the solar system around which the planets revolve. Subsequent Ionians correctly calculated the size of the Earth. They understood the stars to be very distant, that they are created and eventually extinguish, and correctly determined that the magnitude of light from a star determined a star's age and phase of life. This was in the second century BCE.

These Greeks were the forerunners of the scientific method and modern astronomy (http://www.vexen.co.uk/religion/christianity_astronomy.html).

This view of the universe was corroborated by Copernicus, Kepler, Galileo, and Isaac Newton centuries later. But the Church rejected this concept for some fifteen hundred years. The Bible has multiple references to Earth as the immovable center of the universe. Joshua 10:12-13, 2 Kings 20:11, Isaiah 38:8, Isaiah 30:26, Psalm 93...all of them and others contradict what astronomers knew for centuries. Scripture establishes the Earth as the focal point of the universe, with the Sun and planets revolving around it. Stars are set in a firmament above it (Genesis). To believe otherwise was to doubt the Word of God, a heresy.

The Church suppressed Copernican theory and its scientific truths by threat, by house arrest, by accusations of blasphemy. By the end of the eighteenth and beginning of the nineteenth century, truth won out. The Church retreated, begrudgingly accepting that the biblical concept of the universe was, in fact, wrong. No, wait! Not "*wrong*-wrong," just incorrectly interpreted for fifteen hundred years. Yeah, that's it... "incorrectly interpreted."

Fast-forward to the twenty-first century. Among modern-day Christians who believe the biblical concept of the universe to be correct are The Geocentric Bible Foundation of Hugoton, Texas, The Tychonian Society, and Catholic Apologetics International, among others. Devout Christian proponents of biblical geocentrism, some of whom believe that the Copernican heliocentric system is

Satan's deception, have websites that fight proven science.[1]

Now I can hear some more moderate/mainstream Christians protesting, *"But these are fringe crazies; they aren't true Christians. They are misinterpreting scripture. The Bible never said these things, etc., etc., etc."* But they would be wrong. They are in denial. They are apologist liars. There are perhaps millions of American Evangelical Christians who subscribe to the Earth being the center of the universe, center of the solar system, Earth as fixed/non-rotating, etc. These are the devout believers who reject science and accept the Word of God unquestioningly, no matter how stupid, pre-scientific, and deluded their scripture and God might be.

I say *these* are the *true* Christians. They don't pick and choose and mince words about what the Bible says and what it "really means." It means what it says! God doesn't misspeak. He doesn't deceive. These believers talk the talk and walk the walk. These Christians deserve credit for their unfailing, uncompromising acceptance of the inerrant Bible as the Word of God, un-contradictable.

These folks are also complete imbeciles. But how much more so than their brethren who choose to selectively believe in reanimation of dead bodies, virgin pregnancy, walking on water, life after death, demons, angels, heaven, hell, the Second Coming, Original Sin, Noah's Ark, et al, just because the Bible told 'em so? By my calculation, not enough to make much of a difference.

---

[1]   Here are some examples: HTTP://WWW.ENDOFMAN.COM/TRUE_RELIGION/ GALILEOHERESY.HTM, HTTP://WWW.JESUS-IS-LORD.COM/GEOCENTR.HTM, HTTP:// WWW.MBOWDEN.SURF3.NET/, HTTP://WWW.FIXEDEARTH.COM/, HTTP://WWW. GEOCENTRICITY.COM/

23

Racism, Ignorance, and Hate on Loan from God

15 Sep 2009

Last week President Obama went on television to encourage American schoolchildren to stay in school and study hard because it is the path to success and a stronger nation. Period.

The firestorm of vitriol by the fundamentalist religious groups who align with the far right was beyond the pale. Never before in the history of this nation has a US president, the leader of the free world, been so maligned and attacked for an appeal to education. Here are just a few examples of the insanity that was spewed by the religiously afflicted in opposition to President Obama's speech to the kids:

"Public schools can't teach children to speak out in support of the sanctity of human life or traditional marriage. President Obama and the Democrats wouldn't dream of allowing prayer in school. Christmas Parties are now Holiday Parties. But the Democrats have no problem going against the majority of American people and usurping the rights of parents by

sending Pied Piper Obama into the American classroom." Jim Greer, Chairman of the GOP of Florida

The Christian Coalition's blog made the claim that Obama's speech would result in teachers directing school children *"...to do volunteer work in the areas which he is concerned about: going to rallies and getting their parents to go with them to support universal health care; encouraging their Members of Congress to vote for Obama's huge tax increase schemes."*

The fundamentalist OneNewsNow posted several pieces against Obama's speech. One was titled, *"Mother Fears Obama School Speech Will Be 'Indoctrination Into Socialism.'"* Another title screamed *"Obama's School Speech—Social Indoctrination?"*

A 2010 gubernatorial candidate and member of Woodlake Assembly of God, Brogdon said he was worried that Obama might address *"environmental conservation and other social issues. These are topics for parents to talk about with their children, not the President of the United States."*

The founder of the American Family Policy Institute urged parents to boycott the president's speech, accusing Obama of wanting to "brainwash" American schoolchildren and comparing his administration to the *"leaders of the Hitler Youth"* (http://www.ethicsdaily. com/news.php?viewStory=14826).

Look, a long time ago I came to the conclusion that the most religiously infected are the most ignorant and uneducated people on the face of the planet. However, I underestimated their capacity for racism and hate, their knee-jerk reactionary fear response, and their disdain for thought and civility.

Meanwhile, search as I may, I can find no examples of atheists, humanists, agnostics, Muslims, Jews, Hindus,

Satanists, Wiccans, or anyone besides Evangelical Fundamentalist Christians condemning Obama for his wanting
to encourage our children to be educated.

I'm convinced that when they say, *"God's will be
done,"* it means, "God wills you to abandon all dignity
and reason, O ye mind-slaves of superstition."

24

Lessons of the Post-Rapture Pet Rescue Business

19 Sep 2009

What started out as a concept with some money-making opportunity has turned out to be a remarkable educational experience.

Over the past ten weeks since the site began, my business partner, Brad, and I have received two thousand-plus emails from atheists applauding our post-Rapture pet rescue service, *Eternal Earth-Bound Pets* (*http://www.eternal-earthbound-pets.com/*) as "genius," "brilliant," and the funniest poke at fundies they have ever witnessed. Naturally, almost all of them want an opportunity to join the ranks of our rescuer cadre. We have largely demurred thus far and not taken on additional rescuers or expanded our area of coverage. We might have predicted this kind of response, but hardly in the numbers experienced.

Then there are the angry Christians who see this service offering one of three ways:

- Evangelicals who perceive this as ridicule of their sacred belief, for which they assure me I will "burn in hell forever," and who would no more entrust their pet to a godless atheist than they would a Korean restaurant owner. Some try their proselytizing act, assuming the threat of hell would jog my intellect free from my brain and result in shutting down our operation.

- Non-Rapture-believing Christians who are embarrassed by their Rapture-believing brethren assuring me that I will "burn in hell forever" for promulgating this misinterpretation of scripture. Sometimes their email is sprinkled with obscenities that one would think would prohibit their kissing Jesus or their moms with their filthy mouths.

- Christians who insist their pets will be beaming up to Jesus with them and that my ignorance of this proves I am a "fool." Naturally, this is inventive, feel-good doctrine that does not exist anywhere in scripture. But invariably they warn me I will be "burning in hell forever."

As you can see, they all share one common theme: the promise of an eternal camel hump BBQ in the netherworld.

But the letters that surprised me the most were from liberal/moderate Christians who not only see humor in the details of the terms and conditions and contract language, but who actually congratulate us for our creativity and entrepreneurial endeavor—going so far as to wish us luck in our business. And these aren't just rare occurrences.

Last week I received an email from a lovely lady from Michigan, a believer whose husband happens to be a pastor. She made a suggestion about some of our contract language and explained that she and her husband found the site very entertaining. They hoped we were realizing some sales for our efforts. We exchanged emails. I answered some questions about non-belief, my position on the creation of the universe, and the trials and tribulations of raising a two-year-old (she has one now...I had two over a quarter-century ago). She bought my book for her pastor husband today. I expect this to be the beginning of a long-term pen pal relationship.

Early this week an email challenged our site's statement that all our pet rescuers have blasphemed against the Holy Spirit, in accordance with Mark 3:29. The sender asked me to explain exactly how I interpreted Mark 3:29 and how exactly we had blasphemed, to ensure its being the only "unforgivable sin," as described in scripture. So, having not a lot to do other than watch bad TV, I gave him the scriptural interpretation of what made it the unforgivable sin of the Pharisees, followed by my modern-day interpretation of how to blaspheme in order to make it applicable for non-Pharisee/non-believing blasphemers.

He replied quickly, thanking me for my response, and congratulating me on my knowledge and interpretation of scripture. Turned out he is a retired Episcopal priest, bordering on something like agnostic. He wanted to make sure we weren't just pulling the blasphemy guarantee out of our asses. He wished us luck on our business.

There have been many more emails like these from friendly, charming, funny, and supportive believers.

To say I was surprised would be an understatement. I never would have expected such a divergence of perspective of what our offer meant to Christians, such diametrically opposed emotions emanating from people sharing the same religion, such a difference in temperament and tolerance toward a non-believer.

I turned a year older on September 8. I am really old now, but not too old to be educated and pleasantly surprised.

25

Christian Idol Worship: What *Are* They Thinking?

25 Sep 2009

I read recently about some hideously giant cross looming over an interstate in Texas, a report that caused me no small amount of irritation.

What is it with fanatical Christians that impedes their brains from processing that erecting their giant religious symbol doesn't represent their community, state, or nation; it doesn't appease their God; it doesn't put food in the mouths of the poor; it doesn't cause instant conversions; and it doesn't end divisiveness or intolerance. In fact, it actually encourages the last one.

I am forever amazed that these zealous Christians have zero empathy, are unable to put themselves in the place of non-Christians and non-believers, or understand how we feel when such a symbol is imposed on us. It's a wholly good and wonderful thing to these Christians. They can't fathom it being anything else.

But just imagine their outcry if a giant one-hundred-dred-and-ten-foot-tall Islamic crescent, Star of David,

Wiccan totem, statue of Buddha, or effigy of Brahma were erected along an interstate…illuminated, no less. To these Christians that would be just unacceptable, damn un-American. I imagine they would be moved to hysteria, if not violence.

Beyond that there's this: isn't their love of Christ supposed to be within their hearts? Isn't it enough that he "lives within" them? Do they (and we) need to be reminded who they worship, lest they forget, by the sight of a gigantic, grotesque execution device or an overblown idol of their man-god, for whom no physical description exists? What is with the idolatry to which these fanatics seem to be so devoted? How does it differ from the glorification of statues of Zeus, Isis, Moloch, or Baal, etc., which the pagans viewed as the symbol of their deity, if not its very essence?

Then there is the cost. Hundreds of thousands, even millions, have been invested in these monstrosities—and for what? For the edification of the ministers who reap the publicity with which they'll attract more sheeple to their church? As some kind of public declaration of their piety, like modern-day Pharisees? To teach those godless heathens, Jews, Muslims, and pagan peoples a thing or two about their death cult's symbol? To stake their claim to their religion's superior numbers and influence? Could no better use for that money be found?

Sure, people can do what they like on private property. If they want to put a "Mary on the half-shell" next to their garden gnome, fine. They want a manger in their front yard next to their junk car up on cinder blocks, super. They want to paint a face of their imagined man-god on the side of their doublewide, go for it. But when it comes to imposing their grandiose, mega-gargantuan death devises and imaginary man-god graven images on the public, at least use a little discretion and humility.

I'd wager if their Jesus existed, came to Earth, and saw these things glorified in his name, he'd have some really ugly flashbacks then smite those hideous monuments. But since he doesn't exist, I hope someone does it for him.

26

"Atheism Is a Product of Irrationality"

01 Oct 2009

The above was the title of a recent letter to the editor that appeared in our local newspaper.

There has been something of a reader's opinion letter war going on between the very small number of religious extremists in New Hampshire and freethinkers in our state. Barely a week goes by that something really absurd isn't posted by a religionist that provokes a logical and measured response from the large number of godless NH residents.

Here's an extract from a recent offering from one of our religious men of letters:

"To me, atheism is not only a moral evil but a metaphysical evil because, as defined by Thomas Aquinas (1225-1274), evil is the absence in nature of something that ought to be there; for example, it is a physical evil to have been born with only one eye.

"Atheism is a mental evil because the mind does not have the rationality it ought to have. Abdicating all sense of balance, ratio, and proportionality, atheists are irrational because they deny that of which they have no clear idea."

About as backward and topsy-turvy illogical babble as one could imagine. I couldn't just let it go. My response follows:

"In Mr. Cervo's letter of Sept. 24, he exposed the problem inherent in 'theist think.' Indeed, his letter is the quintessential example of the ills of avoidance of secular thought that seem to be the hallmark of the religiously afflicted.

"Missing an eye is a 'physical evil'? Atheism is a 'metaphysical evil'? Lacking belief in supernaturalism is a 'mental evil'? One can practically hear the screams of the heretics under the Inquisition's torture devises clanking away in Mr. Cervo's basement.

"When the absence of delusion and gullibility—and the acceptance of the scientific method and evidence—is defined as irrationality, and when blind belief in supernaturalism born of the imagination of ancient pre-scientific cultists is considered rational, then we truly have not progressed far beyond the Dark Ages. It is the doctrine of a Bizarro World where 'rational = bad, irrational = good—reality = evil, unreality = righteous.'

"I wonder if Mr. Cervo's concept of rationality includes not 'suffer[ing] a witch to live,' attributing a two-headed frog to Satan's handiwork, and plague to God's wrath. That's the rationality religionists have embraced for thousands of years... that's what they call a 'balanced' mind. It would be laughable if it were not so frightening in its implications."

A similar letter, or one of rebuttal, will no doubt appear next week from a devoted Christian apologist. It's sort of like watching the movie *Groundhog Day*, although if groundhogs could talk, they'd likely make more sense than these religionists.

27

Order in the Natural World?"God Did It!"

05 Oct 2009

To some number of hardcore Fundamentalist Christians, it's incomprehensible that a Creator isn't directly in control of what the rest of us understand as natural forces and events.

A Christian I was debating (I use the term "debate" loosely) insisted that it's impossible for the "design" of the universe to have occurred randomly; it's "too ordered," thus proof of God the Creator. Normally I would posit that the universe is hardly ordered; a simple observation of the chaos of astronomical events, earthquakes, tsunamis, etc. would prove that. But I decided to try a different tack. I pointed out that when sand or any granulated material falls out of a bucket in a vacuum thus unaffected by other forces, the random particles fall into a pile that forms an ordered cone every time. If randomness can't form an ordered design, how does he explain that?

His childlike answer: the person emptying the bucket made it happen...thus the person was the cone's "creator." That natural physical forces cause the random falling particles to form into a well ordered and predictable geometric shape was totally lost on him. The concept never even crossed his mind. He could not connect the hypothetical with the actual; he had to revert to a "creator with a bucket did it."

I explained that the resulting cone would have been identical if it had been wind blown sand falling off a cliff into a protected gully, or a slow trickle of sand, or highly mineralized water dripping from a cave ceiling—that the man and the bucket wasn't the salient point at all. But it was lost on him. He couldn't allow that reality to confuse his theistically motivated, absolutist thinking. "The guy with the bucket did it" was all he would say.

Sends shivers up your spine just to realize these people actually walk and drive among us. Ron White said it best: *"You can't fix stupid."*

28

The Camel's Coming-Out Party

10 Oct 2009

Okay, that title is a little misleading. Allow me to clarify.

My wife and I attended a small party with friends last Saturday night. Four other couples attended—all believers. One couple was husband and wife pastors at two local churches with whom my wife is very friendly, having worked with them on a flood disaster recovery project a few years back.

We settled into the living room, sipping champagne, chit-chatting, and eating dessert, when one woman said she had heard I published a book and was curious as to its subject. It was seconded by an *"Oh, you're an author? Yes, tell us about it."*

Echoing in the recesses of my mind is the old saying about never discussing religion or politics at a social event. This holds especially true when surrounded by Christians whose eighteenth- and seventeenth-century predecessors were prone to meting out some pretty severe penalties for non-belief. But this is New Hampshire, not seventeenth-century Salem, Massachusetts. Not being shy about promoting my book, after a nanosecond's hesitation I did my thing.

"You mean to say you don't believe in GOD…why not??" was offered by an incredulous young lady in her early thirties who, it seems, has never knowingly been in the presence of an admitted non-believer. I explained the lack of evidence for any God/gods, my preference toward acceptance of things as real that have a foundation in scientific validity, and my lack of need for a non-physical, supernatural dependency, being a mature self-reliant human in charge of his own destiny, etc., etc.

Parrying with Pascal's Wager, she suggested, *"But wouldn't you be better off believing, just to be safe?"* I explained who Blaise Pascal was and gave her the usual retorts that have blunted that argument so often and over so many years that few theists even bother to use Pascal anymore.

Another woman, in her mid-sixties, jumped in: *"But how do you explain our existence if not for God?"* Which led me to the Big Bang, the primordial soup, the theory of evolution… *"But how could the Big Bang start; it had to have a start…everything has a beginning."* When I said I didn't know—no one does yet, although there are theories—she reverted to, *"Well, that's where God comes in…He started it."*

This led to the discussion of "if everything has a beginning then who or what created God?" Then into the "God of the Gaps," with all of them agreeing that five hundred years ago, when man didn't know what caused lightning to destroy another sect's church, it was assumed that "God did it." When plague struck, "God's wrath did it," etc. Only the atheists did not default to "God" as an explanation; they simply said, "We don't know…yet." But somehow I sensed my audience didn't make the connection between those things and my saying, *"We don't know what caused the Big Bang… yet."* Information overload, perhaps.

None of them, I surmised, save the husband and wife pastors, had read the Bible. Thus, they were disarmed by my references to chapter and verse to emphasize my contentions. In fact, the husband pastor agreed with most of my points, confirming some of the less charming and inexplicably cruel laws of Deuteronomy, the cruel 2 Kings 2 tale of the forty-two children being torn by bears, as well as various verses that have been proven to be less than scientifically accurate.

It was a classic discussion between gentle believer folks who had minimal experience with debate and just as little exposure to a secular, well read, religiously versed person of reality. The discussion followed predictable patterns and themes—after all, there's not much new under the sun when it comes to theist think or defending the faith.

As the evening came to a close, I handed out my book's business cards with that charming camel's picture on it to the delight of the guests. I sensed a good time was had by all; I know I had a ball. Just as we were kissing and shaking hands goodbye, that young lady gave me a hug and whispered, *"You know you're going to hell, don't you?"*

Which proves the old adage, "You can lead a believer to thinking but…" Well, you know the rest.

29

Anne Frank Had It Coming

15 Oct 2009

Anne Frank was fifteen years old when the Nazis discovered her family's hiding place in Amsterdam. She had been hiding behind a false wall in cramped quarters, supplied rations by a sympathetic Christian family for two years before they were found and arrested in 1945.

They were all sent to death camps. Anne died seven months later in Bergen-Belsen concentration camp in Germany after having seen her sister die before her. Her crime was that she was born and raised in the religion of her family. She was Jewish.

Anyone who has read the book or seen the movie *The Diary of Anne Frank* is familiar with the horrific existence this little girl had to endure before and up to her death. They may also recall that her writings exposed innocence, optimism and goodness best exemplified by one line in her diary written in July 1944 while in hiding and living in fear. That one line read: *"In spite of everything, I still believe that people are really good at heart."*

This would be the end of the story of that young girl with no future whose fear and pain we could only imagine. Except, according to Christian doctrine, it doesn't end there. Not by a long shot.

Christian doctrine is very clear, very succinct, and very definitive: the only way to the Father is through the Son. In other words, unless one believes in the divinity of Jesus before they die, they cannot enter heaven and are cast into hell with the rest of the damned. And there, according to Christian tradition, the inmates are tortured endlessly. They burn in a lake of fire. They are tormented by demons. This all lasts for an eternity with no hope of relief. According to Christianity, this is where Anne Frank is now. And for pure entertainment value, believers get to watch Anne's torture from their recliners in heaven. According to Thomas Aquinas, the medieval theologian, "That the saints may enjoy their beatitude and the grace of God more abundantly they are permitted to see the punishment of the damned in hell."

According to this lovely Christian doctrine, Anne is likely rooming with Hitler, Pol Pot, the 9/11 terrorists, and every child molester and mass murder who failed to accept Jesus as his savior before the switch was pulled and electricity coursed through their bodies, extinguishing their despicable lives.

And why? Why is that fifteen-year-old girl who suffered so much in life condemned to an after-life of never-ending suffering? Her crime was that she was born and raised in the religion of her family. She was Jewish.

Some liberal Christians will say they reject that doctrine, that they don't buy into it, that God is a loving god and would never permit such a thing. But that's because they are in denial, preferring not to stare directly into the face of an intolerant, fear-mongering, threatening, and intimidating doctrine that is at the very heart of Christianity.

The True Christians will shrug their shoulders and say, *"God gave her free will. It was her choice to accept or reject Jesus."* In other words, she could have abandoned the faith of her parents, her grandparents, her great-grandparents, etc., simply seen it as a false religion, and come over to Jesus. Failing to do so wasn't God's fault: *"HE didn't condemn her—she condemned herself."* Some of them actually believe what they are saying is reasonable and just. They don't even give it a second thought. Basically they are saying; don't blame God for the acts of this fifteen-year-old Jewess Christ killer.

Others mouth similar, albeit less callous words. They toe the Christian line but are feeling uncomfortable with it. Some will even offer that she may have accepted Jesus while in the death camp and could be with him now. But they know what they are doing. They know they are trying to make the unjust sound just, the unfair sound fair, an inexplicably intolerant and horrific doctrine appear not so bad. They are embarrassed by the very doctrine that they themselves embrace.

And so this innocent Jewish girl, like so many millions of others like her, is victimized twice: first by an inhumane totalitarian state to which murder of the innocent was a right, and then victimized by a religious doctrine to which eternal torture of an innocent is her just desserts. At least the Nazis only killed her once. Christian doctrine has her being tortured forever. Which is the lesser of the two evils?

Yes, Anne Frank had it coming. Just ask a loving Christian, or their loving God.

30

Why Religious Fanatics *Want* to Be Hated

20 Oct 2009

Some time ago I participated in a religious debate chat room on MSN that had as a frequent visitor a patently insane fundamentalist Christian. An admitted schizophrenic sexually abused as a child, she was and likely still is suffering from schizophrenia-induced hyper-religiosity. She called herself "Truth Teller," a remarkably ironic tag.

This woman spoke with God, and God spoke to her. Literally. She spoke on and off in Old English, ala the King James Bible translation, spewing out verse, ranting about *"gnashing of teeth," "all knees will bend," "He will come with a sword in his mouth,"* etc., etc., condemning anyone to Hell, believers and non-believers alike, for failing to believe or interpret scripture as she saw it. She also claimed to despise religion, which meant she hated all other sects/denominations of Christianity except her own personal brand. Her disgust for the "pagan Catholics" was almost as intense as it was for atheists. No matter how often she was dismissed, thrown out, and derided as a troll and provocateur, she kept coming back. She thrived on the agitation she caused and verbal abuse she received for it.

I've met this kind of Internet troll on and off over the years. They have often been fodder for my blog and occasionally provide me the inspiration to investigate various scriptural interpretations and research causes for aberrant extremist behavior among believers.

Recently I came across another Christian who exhibits similar traits. The only hardcore Young Earth Fundamentalist in a discussion group almost exclusively comprised of freethinkers, he seems obsessed with atheists and provoking outrage with inflammatory declarations. Many of the things he says are so extreme, so completely outrageous, and so blatantly stupid that in all likelihood he doesn't recognize that his dialogue does more to discredit Christianity than promote it...but that wouldn't make a difference to him even if he were cognizant of it.

What I have come to realize is that these proselytizing fanatical Christian trolls all have one thing in common: the desire to be hated. They want to be abused. They thrive on having insults thrown at them, their statements discredited, even being banned from a group or chat room. But why? What possible benefit comes from such a mindset? What is the impetus for this behavior? Surprisingly, there is an answer, and it's founded in scripture.

"Blessed are you when men hate you, when they exclude you and insult you and reject your name as evil, because of the Son of Man. Rejoice in that day and leap for joy, because great is your reward in heaven. For that is how their fathers treated the prophets"—Luke 6: 22- 23 (NIV).

Understand how these internet fanatical trolls interpret this verse: by being the one gadfly of illogic and gross ignorance, by offering offensive and irrational statements, they incur the wrath of the thinking unsaved by provoking our insults or by being "excluded," banned, or dismissed. In this way they will be rewarded in heaven like a martyr. By inducing hatred and animosity, they are seeking assurance of eternal salvation. They perceive Luke 6 to be encouraging this behavior.

Fred Phelps' Westboro Baptist Church's extremist actions and position on homosexuality isn't simply based on what gays do behind closed doors being offensive to his God. After all, if God existed and wanted to end homosexuality, he could do so in a second with no assistance from Phelps. No, Fred and his band of followers are feathering their nests in heaven by being despised by every thinking person on the planet.

Intentionally provoking anger and discord isn't what Luke had in mind. But to the unstable fanatic Xtians whose only goal is to attain heaven, whose greatest fear is to be "left behind," this is all perfectly sensible. Annoying and pretty creepy, but then being an annoying creep *is* in the best tradition of religious extremists.

31

If Spiritualism/Religion Is Good for You, How Come It Kills Its Adherents?

23 Oct 2009

Well, it happened again. A flock of New Age spiritualists seeking enlightenment go on a retreat of "self-discovery," where there are "powerful Earth energies," pay cash to their guru, step into a sweat lodge, and promptly keel over. Three die; many more are sickened.

According to survivors' reports, people were feeling nauseous, passing out, and wanted to leave. But the self-help guru James Arthur Ray, self-proclaimed "spiritual warrior," insisted they stay inside for their own inner strength.

In the aftermath, Ray coordinates a communication between the dead followers and a "channeler," who assures the survivors that the dead are happy where they are and didn't want to come back. How comforting...and convenient. The survivors didn't buy it. Finally.

It's not as though this is the first time in recent history that the willfully deluded seeking spiritual enlightenment put their trust in a charismatic spiritual leader and are led like lambs to slaughter.

- Guyana – Jim Jones (Christian)
- Waco - David Koresh (Christian)
- Heavens Gate - Marshal Applewhite (Christ delusion nut)
- Order of the Solar Tradition- Luc Jouret (Christian mixed nut)

Those religious sects, cults, and spiritual groups, plus the murders of children and family members at God's behest, have chalked up over thirteen hundred corpses. This latest debacle won't be the last time, either.

There is this thing about people who abandon self-reliance, reality, and common sense, preferring instead to entrust their lives and money to someone who is on a "higher plane of consciousness," is in touch with his "inner spiritualism," or who professes a special relationship with God in pursuit of something beyond reality. You'd think in this day and age they'd be a little more skeptical, a little less gullible, a tad less malleable. But they are believers and superstionalists, which, by definition, means they are gullible and dependent.

It seems that being spiritual or religious is a prerequisite to being gently lulled into suicide by a shamanic shepherd. When was the last time anyone heard of mass suicide at a meeting of non-believer National Academy of Science fellows at the behest of the head of the academy? Or an atheist organization drinking cyanide-laced Kool Aid during a family outing? Or

MENSA members collectively subjecting themselves to life-threatening conditions at the say-so of a MENSA group leader? You haven't and you won't. What sets we the thinking apart from the spiritually dependent and religiously oriented dirt-nap candidates is trust in reality, self-reliance, and discernment. If only it could be bottled and sold.

32

Why Religionists Can't Take Non-Belief for an Answer

27 Oct 2009

I caught a glimpse of Oprah's show the other evening while waiting for the early news to come on. Let me be clear—I never watch Oprah or her spawn, Dr. Phil. I'm not a fan. I'll leave it at that lest I inadvertently alienate some of my beloved readers.

Oprah was in Denmark for reasons I didn't catch. The first thing I heard was her thoughtful observation that practically everyone on the street was blond. Imagine that: blondes in Denmark! (One wonders, were she in Botswana, if she would comment on the abundance of people with black hair.)

As she chatted with two tall, thirtyish, attractive, and definitely blond women who seemed to be her unofficial tour guides, the subject turned to religion. The conversation went something like this (paraphrasing):

Oprah: "What about religion? Are you religious, do you attend church?"

Blonde A: "No, I am not religious. The churches around here are usually empty."

Blonde B: "I do not believe in God. Many here are non-believers."

Oprah: "Well, maybe you believe in God but just don't realize it?"

Blondes A&B: [Blank stare—awkward hesitation]

Blonde A: [Feeling the need to throw Oprah a bone and trying not to cause her unnecessary embarrassment] "Maybe there is a higher power of some kind. Who is to know?"

Oprah: "Maybe you are not religious but just spiritual?"

Blondes A&B: [Blank stare]

Blonde B: "Maybe."

Oprah: [Nods approvingly]

"Spiritual!?" Oh shit!

Mrs. Hump and I looked at each other with incredulity at this peculiar line of questioning. What exactly was that all about? Why was Oprah so insistent? Why was she adamant that two Danes who openly reject religious superstition, as do so many European countries, most notably Denmark (which is among the least religious countries on the planet), *must* believe or *may* believe in God but are evidently too stubborn or stupid to realize it?

Why was this so important to her that she twice attempted to eek out some confirmation of belief, contrive a convoluted connection to, or validation of, her own enslavement to superstition? I found this bizarre and yet so typical of the pomposity of Americans of faith. I'm sure the blond Danes found it quite strange. It was clear they found it uncomfortable.

I just wish it had been me she was sermonizing to about believing. My response would have been somewhat less genteel: *"No, you self-absorbed theist refugee from reality. What part of 'I'm an ATHEIST' don't you understand!?"*

It seems Oprah, as an American theist just can't come to terms with the fact that the stranglehold that Christianity held on Europe for a thousand years has been broken. She/they don't want to acknowledge it. Perhaps it's because that fact looms like a specter of the inevitable that they'd prefer not to acknowledge. Or perhaps it's because delusion loves company.

33

How about Just a Little Theist Integrity?

02 Nov 2009

I've been visiting a blog by an ex-pastor, now agnostic. He posts some good, thought-provoking articles. Recently he blogged about a mother whose daughter joined a Christian denomination that has a theology the mom finds a bit extreme, causing a rift in their relationship. She asked the agnostic ex-pastor blogger to pray for her daughter to come to her senses and return to the fold, or at least not abandon her familial relationships in favor of this Christian "cult." This presents an obvious dilemma to the blogger, who no longer believes in a deity or in prayer.

One of his readers posted this advice: *"I've never seen any verifiable miracle answers to prayer, I would pray for her and her daughter simply because she asked me to. If she believes in prayer, then I would believe in it too for her sake. This is what friends do with or without all the theology."*

I don't know what to make of this. The reader-commenter is a self-described "Christ-Centric-Deist." Presumably this means he holds Jesus in reverence but without imbuing him with god qualities while believing in a Creator of the universe, who no longer is involved with his creations' daily lives. With an absent Creator, prayer is viewed as meaningless. But whatever his belief, the statement has the unmistakable stench of religionist hypocrisy.

So let me ask: if a friend of yours practiced witchcraft and he put faith in the sacrifice of a chicken, would you sacrifice a chicken on his behalf if he asked you to? And could you "believe" in its efficacy for his sake, because that is what friends do with or without sharing the same delusional theology?

If a friend was Pentecostal and asked you to pray over her dying child, who could easily be saved by modern medicine, would you pray with her or convince her to take the child for medical help? If she refused, would you "accept her belief" or would you notify the authorities, even if it were painful for your friend?

How does practicing a superstitious ritual, with no scientific basis or evidence for efficacy, one that you do not imbue with credibility, genuinely benefit the person making the request? Doesn't doing that violate one's principles? Isn't it tantamount to hypocrisy/a deception? Doesn't it lend credence to/reinforce a superstition that has no validity, but gives false hope of a positive result to the superstitiously afflicted?

Wouldn't we be simply placating someone with a condescending gesture by masquerading as a like believer for their short-term/immediate sense of relief and hope, when all along we know it yields no possibility of real long-term relief or resolution? Isn't it like saying: *"Reality is okay for me, but you lack the ability to deal with reality, so I'll come down to your level and pretend in order to make you feel better for the moment. Aren't I magnanimous?"*

A friend who is honest, has integrity, and is true to their own position would say:

"I can't deceive you and participate in a gratuitous ritual in which I hold no belief; I respect you too much for that. But I love you and will help you in real and meaningful ways."

Religious belief is already based on a lie. A real friend doesn't heap one irrational lie on another...no matter how one tries to justify/rationalize it. Maybe this kind of deception of self and others is something theists have trained themselves to do. Frankly, I could never prostitute my intellect, integrity, or honesty to legitimize a person's feel-good delusion.

34

Flag Ceremony Co-Opted by Religionists: Is Nothing Secular Sacred?

08 Nov 2009

I read today that during an upcoming Veteran's Day service conducted by a Catholic church, they are going to recite *"The Meaning of the Twelve Folds of Our Flag."* Having never heard of this, I decided to do some investigation. I suspected the worst and I wasn't surprised.

It seems the traditional formal flag-folding ceremony, which entails twelve folds of the flag, culminating in a triangular shape with just the stars showing, has been mysteriously imbued with religious significance, specifically Christianity.

Here is the recitation of "the meaning" of the twelve folds of the American flag:

1. First fold of our American Flag is a symbol of life.
2. Second fold is a symbol of **our belief in the eternal life.**

3. Third fold is made in honor and remembrance of the veterans who have departed their prospective ranks, who gave a portion of their life for the defense of our country, to attain peace throughout the world, not to have been in vain and shall never be forgotten.

4. Fourth fold represents our weaker nature, for, as American citizens **trusting in God**, it is **to Him we turn** in times of peace as well as in times of war for **His divine guidance**.

5. Fifth fold is a tribute to our country, for in the words of the immortal Stephen Decatur, "Our country, in dealing with other countries, may she always be right, but it is still our country, right or wrong."

6. Sixth fold of our flag represents where our hearts lie—and it is with our hearts that we pledge allegiance to the flag of the United States of America, and to the republic for which it stands, one nation **under God**, indivisible, with liberty and justice for all.

7. Seventh fold is a tribute to our armed forces, for it is through these same armed forces that our country is protected and our flag protected against all her enemies, whether they be found within or without the boundaries of our republic.

8. Eighth fold is a tribute to the one who entered into the **Valley of the Shadow of Death,** that we might see the light of the day, and this fold is made to honor a mother, for whom it flies on Mother's Day.

9. Ninth fold is a tribute to womanhood, for it has been through their **faith**, love, loyalty, and devo-

tion that the characters of men who have made this country great have been molded.

10. Tenth fold is a tribute to fathers, for they too have given of their sons and daughters for the defense of our country since they were his first born.

11. Eleventh fold of our flag, for in the eyes of a **Hebrew citizen,** this represents the lower portion of the seal of **King David and King Solomon,** and glorifies in their eyes **the God of Abraham, the God of Isaac and the God of Jacob.**

12. Twelfth and final fold, for in the eyes of a **Christian citizen, this represents an emblem of eternity and glorifies in their eyes God the Father, God the Son and God the Holy Ghost**.

One might ask:

- *"Where in the Flag Code is this religiously infused script written?"* It isn't.
- *"When did Congress sanction this religious interpretation of a simple, traditional flag-folding ceremony?"* It didn't.
- *"Is it a tradition going back to some earlier time?"* Nope.
- *"Is the military using this religious script at any official ceremonies?"* No.
- *"Would governmental sanction of such an interpretation be a violation of the First Amendment Establishment Clause?"* Clearly.
- *"Might not this be offensive to any non-Jewish/non-Christian veteran who fought for that flag and served their country?"* It is to me.

So why is it that this non-inclusive, alienating, totally fabricated, and unauthorized infusion of Judeo-Christian religiosity into a wholly secular ritual has magically appeared? It seems some theists must infect everything with their cultist-think and take every opportunity to equate their religion with patriotism.

If I'm ever at a ceremony where my service as a veteran is being recognized and some religionist invokes that fictitious, insulting, and fraudulent religious drivel in an attempt to wrap Christ in our flag, they had better be prepared for a raging camel...for verily defecation will hit the fan.

35

Befuddled God: Good Thing He Has So Many Interpreters

13 Nov 2009

Their God, it seems, is an inarticulate and confused old fool who has to rely on his creations to figure out and explain exactly what his words mean and policies should be. Liken it to a ninety-eight-year-old senile company founder who is kept locked in his office by the board of directors, and who translate his babble into whatever the board wants it to mean to the shareholders.

The evidence for this is overwhelming.

I had previously mentioned the belief of some Christians that once they go to heaven, the perks include being able to watch the suffering of those souls condemned to hell. I myself have been on the receiving end of this taunt by religious fanatics who anticipate with great glee this marvelous side benefit of heavenly residence.

The basis for this belief is their (and Saint Thomas Aquinas') interpretation of Luke 16:19-31. In it a rich man in hell converses with and is seen by Abraham in heaven. It's either interpreted as a parable or a real event, depending on the myth receptors of fanatical conservative Xtians...or what their sect leaders tell them.

A theist in a message group I frequent took issue with my reference to this interpretation. Evidently I made this all up. I was wrong. Never mind that he has had no interaction with any with those fundies who interpret Luke 16 in this way; he has even less understanding that biblical verse has been interpreted in different ways ever since the Church stopped making possession of the Bible and independent interpretation of it a capital offense.

The Reformation, which led to a multitude of breakaway Christian sects from the Catholic Church, was in response to disagreement with Catholic dogma and scriptural interpretation. Today there are an estimated twenty-eight thousand different denominations and sects of Christianity. More added regularly. Not one of them interprets every chapter and verse the same way.

Some of these sects reject the Trinity; others reject the existence of a physical hell. Some believe the ingestion of the wine and wafer is truly eating the body of Christ; others believe it is just symbolic. Some believe all those who never hear the "Word" and thus are unfamiliar with Jesus go to hell for their ignorance; others believe they are saved. Some believe in the Rapture; others reject it. Some Rapture-believers think the seven years of Tribulation happen before the Rapture; others that it happens after the Rapture. Some believe God literally dictated the Bible; others that it was inspired by God. Some believe in Universal

Reconciliation; most believe in damnation to hell for non-believers. There is even a worldwide movement of Evangelicals who believe that Highway 35 that runs from Texas to Minnesota is "the Holy Highway" as described in Isaiah 35:8 (http://wcco.com/bridgecollapse/holy.highway.movement.2.602358.html).

This is just the tip of the iceberg. There are hundreds if not thousands of other concepts and interpretations of "God's Word" and his expectations that distinguish a Calvinist from a Lutheran, from a Methodist, from a Quaker, from a Shaker, from a Mennonite, from a Baptist, from a Santeria practitioner, from a Jehovah's Witness, from a Mormon, from a Christadelphian, from a Kimbanguist, etc., etc., ad nauseam. These sects and denominations can't even all agree on the order of the Ten Commandments or their precise meanings.

But what they all share in common is scriptural "evidence" for their conflicting viewpoints.

So with all the confusion of the scripture, the inarticulate ranting, what's a true believer and devout Christian to do? Simple—make the words mean that which is most expedient and supports his agenda. Don't wait around for God to unscramble and reedit his indecipherable, open-ended, contradictory babble. He's already had a few thousand years to do that and seems to have lost interest or capability. So his creations have to do it for him, in thousands of differing ways. Basically, a cluster flock of self-appointed God interpreters.

Of course, if they don't like any of the interpretations, they can just branch off—start their own sect based on what God and the Bible *really* mean. Have lots of wives, handle snakes, roll around on the floor babbling incoherently, kill gays, hole up in a compound and collect weaponry, or move to a jungle and feed their followers cyanide-laced Kool Aid. It's all good. The Bible tells them so.

36

Religion in the News: A Busy Fortnight for the Righteous

17 Nov 2009

I don't usually write about the continuous flow of reports on pastors, priests, youth ministers, and their followers' predilection for criminality, perversion, etc. I may reference it to make a point or to underscore a contention, but I don't commonly write about it; it's too frequent and too widely reported in the media.

But the past two weeks have been a high-water mark for religious obscenity. It's hard to ignore the contribution theists have made to current events over the past fourteen days. Top news stories included:

- A devout **American-born Muslim US Army major** at Fort Hood, Texas, shouted, "Allah Akbar" or some such variation of the Islamic praise of God, and opened fire on a room full of unarmed people, killing thirteen of his American soldier comrades and wounding thirty others.

- The **Reverend Fred Phelps**, of the Westboro Baptist Church, has now decided promoting hatred against gays isn't enough to satisfy God, and has branched out into anti-Semitism (http://www.usatoday.com/news/religion/2009-11-13-westboro-gay-jewish_N.htm).
- The **Catholic diocese of Washington, D.C.** has lovingly threatened to shut down adoption and healthcare services and services for the homeless if Washington, D.C. doesn't stop protecting homosexuals from discrimination (http://www.washingtonpost.com/wp-dyn/content/discussion/2009/11/12/DI2009111208573.html).
- **Phillip Garrido,** kidnapper and child-rapist of Jaycee Dugard, was the founder of a church he called "God's Desire." He had been a devout Jehovah's Witness and preached the word of God to his captive daily. He now claims Christ has cured him of his sexual perversion (http://www.foxnews.com/story/0,2933,549600,00.html).
- **Evangelist Tony Alamo**, founder of Alamo Ministries, was sentenced to one hundred and seventy-five years in prison for taking girls as young as nine years old over state lines for sex (http://www.religionnewsblog.com/).
- Twenty-one new claims of clergy sex abuse have been filed against the **Catholic Diocese of Spokane** (http://www.spokesman.com/stories/2009/nov/03/diocese-hit-with-21-new-claims/).

Yes, it's been a busy two weeks for religionists here in America. One wonders where they find the time to pray, eat man-god flesh wafers, and deny evolution. If we looked worldwide at the list of crimes, hypocrisy, perversity, and despicable hatred promulgated by the God-fearing devout of all religions, and with their god's blessing, they would likely fill a dozen pages.

And what do the religionists say about their believer brethren who make the headlines? *"Oh, they aren't True Christians"; "Oh, he wasn't practicing True Islam."* As usual, it's simple denial. That's what they do best.

But, to be fair, and in full disclosure, here is a list of crimes, hate, hypocrisy, and perversion promulgated by those unethical, amoral, hell-bound, and godless American atheists, agnostics, and freethinkers, and their organizations, over the past two weeks:

-
-
-
-
-
-

And that's just the tip of the iceberg.

37

"Hey, Little Suzie Is Having a Tourette's Episode! Who's up for an Exorcism?"

26 Nov 2009

A little recent history is in order:

- Oct. 22, 2009: An eighteen-year-old Virginia woman **died** during a Korean **exorcism** intended to evict demons or other spiritual entities.
- October 2007: An **exorcism** in Wellington, New Zealand led to the **death** of a woman and the hospitalization of a teen.
- July 29, 2007: Phoenix, Arizona, officers responding to a report of an **exorcism** on a three-year-old girl found her grandfather **choking her,** and used stun guns to subdue the man, who later died, authorities said Sunday.
- Jun 21, 2005: A Romanian priest and four nuns have been charged in the **death** of a reportedly schizophrenic nun who was **crucified in an exorcism**.
- July 9, 2004: A Milwaukee, Wisconsin, preacher was found guilty in an eight-year-old boy's 2003 **exorcism death.**

- March 2000: In Emeryville, California, five members of a small Christian religious group have been charged with the beating **death** of a twenty-five-year-old Korean woman, who police say was killed during an **exorcism** ceremony to "cast out her *demons*."

This is just the "advertised" craziness. The majority of these kinds of stories are below the surface, hidden away, sometimes sanctioned by the Church, quietly practiced by the religiously devout. To them, demons are as real as your UPS man. Demons infect humans and it's up to them to exorcise them. The power of Christ compels them, it seems.

Exorcisms pre-date Christianity and were practiced by the ancient Jews. But they gave it up long ago. Christians just don't seem to be able to break the habit. After all, what was sauce for their divine goose, Jesus, is sauce for the modern-day Christian quack shamanic gander. Let modern understanding of brain malfunction and psychiatric conditions and their treatments be damned! This is Satan's handiwork and the religiously afflicted and mentally constipated aren't going to stand by and watch Satan win THIS soul, no siree Bob!

Not just your Old World Catholic great-grandmother's mumbo jumbo anymore, exorcisms are also sanctioned and practiced by a variety of Protestant sects: Anglicans, Lutherans, Methodists, and Pentecostals... possibly others. There are also the do-it-yourself exorcists who jump into action at the first sign of a loved one's demonic possession (a la Gov. Bobby Jindal of Louisiana who presided over an exorcism of his then fiancée). Then there are the freelance exorcists happy to ply their trade and cast out those little demons from those little devils for the right price. They're just doing the Lord's work.

What we don't know, what the media never reports, are how many mentally challenged children and adults are subjected to this religiously inspired ritual madness, survive, but whose conditions are exacerbated by the pain and mental stress of forced physical abuse, deprivation, rattle-shaking, and incantations of these throwback practitioners of pre-scientific ancient ignorance. Jesus Honking Christ, people, it's the twenty-first century and the civilized world, not the sixth century or the jungles of Borneo!

Like the dirty little non-secret of clergy child molestation, exorcism is kept under wraps by the clergy. Oh, they enjoy doing both those things, but it best be kept quiet, practiced discretely behind closed doors...and only by those endowed with "special training."

I can picture them dressed in their special costumes, readying their demon-extracting paraphernalia, throwing back a double shot of Johnny Walker, and whispering to the semi-lucid, restrained, and frightened victim: *"Don't tell anyone. It'll be our little secret. It won't hurt too much...besides, God wants me to do this."* I understand in many religious circles that phrase has multiple applications and is used all too frequently.

38

"Where Are All the People?" The Young Earth Argument from Ignorance

05 Dec 2009

One of the worst-thought-out arguments for Young Earth Creationism is that the current population of the planet is just not large enough to support an Old Earth. It's a fundamentalist apologetic predicated on the concept that if man's appearance on Earth was very much older than the biblically calculated six to ten thousand years, the population of the planet would be monumentally larger than the 6.8 billion people we currently have. Q.E.D., the planet can only be six to ten thousand years old.

The math, logic, and (no surprise here) understanding of birth rates and fertility as influenced by food availability, dramatic changes in human aging/

longevity, infant/child mortality rates, et al, is so lacking as to be laughable. Just a little research would enlighten most people. Here are just a very few anecdotal statistics out of hundreds of scientifically supported examples:

- The average life span from the Neolithic age to medieval Europe averaged eighteen to twenty-five years old.[1]
- Seventy-five percent of children born in London between 1730 and 1749 died before the age of five.
- In Zurich, a cemetery that was in use between the ninth and twelfth centuries shows that 50 percent of those interred had died before the age of eighteen.
- In Britain, a sixth-century cemetery at Cannington reflects 64 percent of its residents died before age eighteen.[2]
- Child mortality in France, as late as the early eighteenth century, was 45 percent between the first and fifth years of age alone.[3]
- In the hunter/gatherer societies of the Paleolithic age, fertility rates varied as food supplies increased or declined. Their reproductive spans were short, and it is estimated that 80 percent-plus of children died within the first five years. [4]

---

1   http://en.wikipedia.org/wiki/Life_expectancy

2   Julia M. H. Smith, *Europe after Rome: A new cultural history, 500-1000*, page 66

3   Thomas Cragin, Murder in Parisian Streets: Manufacturing crime and justice in the Popular, page 245

4   http://www.cas buffalo.edu/classes/apy/mcelroy/medapy01/exercise4b.html

Of course, none of this speaks to sub-Saharan populations whose child mortality rates even today are horrendous, never mind what they were tens of thousands of years ago. And never mind the widespread famines and plagues, the latter of which accounted for the decimation of upwards of 50 percent of Europe's population in the 1300s plague event alone. In fact, it wasn't until the early twentieth century that the average lifespan reached thirty-five to forty years old. Only in the past few decades did human life span reach an average of 65 years old.

The bottom line is that population growth is a brand-new phenomenon, relatively speaking. Earth went from one billion people in 1750 to six billion in 2000; that's <u>a population growth of five billion only in the past two hundred and fifty years.</u>

But all this is mind-boggling and way too involved for your average Christian Young Earther. Besides, facts just make their heads hurt. They neither need nor want facts, objective science, or forensic evidence. It's enough to just toss out the statement, *"Where are all the people?"* for the most backward sheep to "baa" in lemming-like unison.

I've actually seen that fundie argument proffered three times. Each time I explained about the factors that impacted population growth since Homo sapiens appeared some two hundred thousand years ago. Two of the fundamentalists admitted they didn't know anything about those things nor cared about them. Of the two, only one had a high school education. They simply took it off a fundamentalist website and accepted it as "gospel." They likely still do and will pass on the disinformation to their off spring..

The third proponent attempted to provide proof that scientists and anthropologists have confirmed this "not enough people" argument, stating that even they were baffled as to why we have a population of "so few when there should be so many more." Naturally, these "scientists" accepted the Young Earth Creation myth as a result. It didn't take long to find out the scientists and anthropologists in question were unaccredited and/or were YEC fundamentalists employed by YEC fundamentalist foundations. No surprise there.

This is what passes for truths to those who will grasp at anything, distort and ignore volumes of corroborated historical research, and invent support for their unsupportable religio-science. And all along they know their eagerly accepting audience lacks the intellect and curiosity necessary to learn the truth about human development.

Whenever I hear this kind of idiocy I have to remind myself it's the twenty-first century…

…for most of us.

39

Crediting God, Chance, or Self-Determination: Hump "Witnesses" for Reality

09 Dec 2009

> *"I cannot comprehend the things that happen in my life being due to chance...if there is proof that these cannot be God's influence or that He doesn't exist I am willing to consider it."*

My Christian pen pal, the pastor's wife, wrote the above after recapping for me some good results, predominantly financial, that emerged from some recent unfortunate circumstances in her life. She credits God. My response to her follows:

Dear M,

I do not credit chance with everything in life. I do credit chance with some number of things. The fact is we influence our life, and whether we capitalize on those chance occurrences is often up to us. Let me give you an example.

I graduated college with a BA in psychology and a minor in religion. I had no idea what I was going to do after graduation. So I went to campus interviews with every company that I could, receiving employment offers mostly from insurance companies and retail companies. I picked retail because my father was a retail executive all his life. I had no particular interest in retail management but I had some idea what it was.

Neither fate, nor chance, nor the influence of the supernatural played any role. It was simply the fact that my BA in psych qualified me for nothing more in the business world than an entry-level position in management. The retail and insurance industries would take people with any BA degree and a mediocre 3.0+ GPA.

I was assigned to a really effective manager mentor who taught me the ropes. But I brought with me an innate skill set: a sense of urgency, a forceful persona, an analytical bent, and a dreadful fear of failure. I excelled in my assignments. I was promoted often, given progressively greater responsibility, and succeeded in most every challenge. My income rose proportionately and faster than many of the MBAs the company hired from more prestigious schools.

Chance played a role in who became my role model. Had I been assigned to a lesser manager—uncaring, inept—perhaps my advancement would have been slowed; maybe not.

My upbringing was responsible for my other qualities and attributes. Certainly had I not been raised by upper-middle-class, non-religious, educated parents who were achievement-oriented and success-driven, who taught me personal responsibility and self-reliance, it's more than likely my business career would have been negatively influenced. Chance determined who my parents were, and what my socio-economic status was; I could not influence either.

I was successful enough that I could easily retire at fifty-five years old and not have to work to support my wife and me. But it wasn't chance/luck that allowed me to retire early. I invested well. My education, my understanding of human behavior, served me well. I learned quickly. I established personal goals and targets. I worked long hours, often six days a week. I hired the best people. I shared my knowledge, developed people's skills. I took certain risks and made innovative changes that cemented my credibility with the organization. I understood corporate politics, albeit I was often a maverick. Based on a combination of chance, personal qualities, and decision-making grounded in logic and intellect, I was able to significantly influence, if not entirely control, my career destiny.

I can account for how each and every stage of my development and business success was influenced by chance, or by my upbringing, or by my own initiative. Not a jot or tittle of supernatural influence is in play. I expect the result would have been the same had I gone into insurance, real estate, or manufacturing.

Perhaps you'd still credit all that to a higher power. I'd guess you'd protest that you need "proof to the contrary" that a higher power didn't influence who my parents were, or influence my business life, and manage my career for some "greater purpose." In fact, I'd wager that as you read this, you are compelled to look at each detail and put it into surpernaturalistic interventional terms. I attribute that to your religious indoctrination and a sense of dependency and helplessness that upbringing imparts.

I can't possibly prove that no supernatural influence exists, just as I can't prove that leprechauns, alien abductions, ghosts, or Thor don't exist. You could not disprove that a being that resembles a squid isn't seated in my parlor as I type this if I were to make such a contention. No one can prove imaginary things don't exist, and why bother? It is a futile and non-productive exercise. But not being able to disprove the imagined doesn't make these things real by default, or suggest they are acting upon or influencing anything.

Some people dismiss chance, self-reliance, personal accountability, and the impact of life's cumulative experiences, preferring to credit all outcomes to powers from the great beyond. It brings to mind the ancients who attributed war, famine, and every other natural event, good fortune, or calamity to supernatural influences. Such people lack the confidence and self-respect to credit their achievements to their own positive attributes and luck, or acknowledge that their failures are due to chance, bad decisions, and/or their own inadequacies. It's too clear, too personal, too simple, and too real. Their lot in life "must" be in the hands of something else, an unseen spirit—an uncontrollable influence—anything but their own hands, mind, and chance.

I went to Vietnam after almost flunking out my first year at school. When I came home from Nam, people said: *"God must have been watching over you; it's a miracle you weren't killed."* But they spoke from ignorance and superstition. The reality was that of all the people who served in Vietnam, "only" ("only" is a horrible word here, but the only one that fits) fifty-eight thousand died out of the two million one hundred thousand who served. That's less than 3 percent fatalities. My odds/chance of being killed were higher as an infantry-rifleman, but even then comparatively small at perhaps 5 to 10 percent.

God/gods had nothing to do with my survival. Miracles didn't save me, nor was it God's will that killed the evangelical Christian sitting across from me in the bunker, who was so busy praying he forgot to keep his head down and reload and fire his rifle. To those theists who like to say, "*Well, God had a purpose for saving you,*" I respond, "Then your god must not believe in itself since evidently his purpose was for me to help bring as many theists as possible to their senses." An explanation every bit as rational as their postulation.

The "reason" or "greater purpose" for that Christian kid and thousands like him dying resides only in the imagination of religionists. The only "reason" is that some people die in war; nothing supernatural about it. Shit occurs.

But what can convince an indoctrinated believer that supernaturalism isn't an influence in everything they do, or that happens, or is done to them? Reason, logic, and analysis of influences—cause and effect—are replaced by "*God did it*" by those who accept supernaturalism over reality. That will change only through the evolution of thinking, and the extinction of myth dependency. It's coming.

40

"Youth Pastor Wanted": Gump Was Right—Stupid Is As Stupid Does

13 Dec 2009

"*Celebration Family Church is looking for a self-motivated leader with a **passion for preschool and elementary age children**... Children's Ministries Director will be responsible for overseeing, **leading and guiding Children's Ministry, which focuses on infants – 8th grade**"*

(http://www.youtube.youthpastor.com/jobs/index.cfm/ Youth Pastor Director Minister Coordinator Fort Myers FL 10337.htm).

The above ad (bold emphasis mine) for a youth pastor position nearly dislodged my hump. It reminded me of those funny headlines Jay Leno reads on his show...you know, the kind that make you say, "*What were they thinking?!*"

Given the nationwide epidemic of clergy pedophilia with a goodly number of youth ministers/pastors among them, you'd think the folks at the Celebration Family Church might have used slightly different phraseology. But my guess is they are completely oblivious to the implications of a clergyman who *has "a passion for preschool and elementary age children."* Of course, I'm giving them the benefit of the doubt by assuming they have been living in a vacuum-sealed bubble for the past twenty years, are comatose, or are simply imbeciles. The alternative would be to suggest they are actually encouraging pedophiles to apply—a front for NAMBLA.

Some irate Christian reading this will no doubt feel the need to defend this ironic and patently dumb ad's wording. They will accuse me of being puerile at best, or a lascivious degenerate at worst. After all, "passion" has many meanings of a nonsexual nature. But that's just denial, something Christians are trained to do. The reality is clergy molestation has dominated the news for years. Just do a Google Images search for "youth pastor minister molesters" and the crowded gallery of faces will disgust you. One would have had to have just hatched from an egg not to see the unfortunate inference in that ad's wording and not be stunned by its insensitivity or obliviousness.

I would be remiss if I did not make an observation about the last sentence in the advertisement. Exactly what does a church person do with infants as it relates to "leading and guiding" them? Lead and guide them to what? When my sons were infants, Mrs. Hump and I pretty much led them to open their mouths for their "flying airplane" baby food spoon, and guided them not to use their feces for modeling clay. Somehow I don't get the impression that food and feces is the focus of a youth ministry's guidance. Evidently the concept of *"get 'em while they're young and moldable"* is a common theme for both religious pedophiles and religious indoctrinators...both of which are criminal, or should be.

41

Oral Roberts Dead at 91:
Obituary for an Iconic Shaman

15 Dec 2009

Oral Roberts died today. Let me say right off that I will not be donning black, buying Mass cards, sitting Shiva, lighting candles, or otherwise mourning the passing of this charlatan and purveyor of the religion virus to the masses. Fact is, as far as I am concerned, Oral was forty years late for his funeral.

This may sound a bit harsh, but I never claimed to be John Donne—any man's death does *not* necessarily diminish me.

Among the nation's earliest televangelists, Oral made a name for himself attracting an enormous following. Although a few years too late to be the inspiration for the ne'er-do-well false prophet evangelical minister in Sinclair Lewis' *Elmer Gantry*, he well could have been.

Oral's claim to fame is epic:

- In the '30s he was a traveling tent healer who shouted abuse at the ill and crippled when they failed to respond to his healing touch.

- In 1977 Roberts claimed to have had a vision from a nine-hundred-foot-tall Jesus, who told him to build the City of Faith Medical and Research Center (a faith and medicine hybrid concept) and that the hospital would be a success. Built in 1980, it closed its doors in 1989. Giant Jesus lied.
- In January 1987, during a fundraising drive, Roberts announced to a television audience that unless he raised eight million dollars by that March, God would "call him home"...i.e., "Gimme money or you're going to kill me." He sucked $9.1 million out of his obedient and fearful sheep.
- Oral announced that through the Roberts ministry, God had raised the dead. His son Richard claimed to have witnessed his father bringing a dead child back to life. The kid was never named.
- He was forced to resign from the presidency of Oral Roberts University due to some funky business about the use of university funds for personal and political purposes.

(Read all about his illustrious career here: http://en.wikipedia.org/wiki/Oral_Roberts.)

He was a pioneer of sorts, paving the way for the legions of despicable, bombastic, fanatical religious shaman—con men, hypocrites, and buffoons all. Men who have made it their life's work to heap more lies upon the undereducated, fleece the gullible, make promises they could never keep, sell the snake oil of belief, and earn millions doing it.

Perhaps millions will mourn Roberts' passing. But not I. That's not to say I wouldn't want to honor him. Given the opportunity, I would gladly pour a bottle of eighteen-year-old Glenfiddich scotch over his grave...as long as he doesn't mind if it passes through my bladder first.

42

Reflections on an Atheist's Christmas

19 Dec 2009

As Christmas rapidly approaches, it would be easy to drag out the usual atheist harangue about Christmas having been co-opted from pagan winter solstice rites, about the pagan roots of the Xmas tree and Yule log, about how the traveling to Bethlehem story to be taxed/counted in a census was nonsensical and antithetical to Roman logic, etc., etc. But while all that would be factually correct, rehashing it would be as interesting as watching *Charlie Brown's Christmas* for the forty-fifth time or, worse, listening to Alvin and the Chipmunks while trapped in an elevator.

Instead, something I saw posted on Facebook by an atheist caught my attention. It said this: *"Ugh, it's Christmas, the most annoying time of year for an atheist."*

I pondered that for a few seconds and found myself in total disagreement. More than that, I couldn't even understand how anyone could be annoyed by Xmas… well, besides store salespeople, UPS drivers, postal workers, and JW's, who view the celebration of Xmas as an abomination. What is it about a gift-giving winter holiday that could make an atheist "annoyed"?

My earliest memory of Xmas and the excitement it heralded was as a four-year-old. My parents were non-practicing Jews. Perhaps "theist-lite" would be a good descriptor. But they always celebrated a secular Xmas for the kids, as well as giving us one gift a night for each of the eight nights of Hanukah.

My mother brought my brother and me to the department store Santa with our wish list. We didn't have a Xmas tree (that was for the "goyim"), but we did hang stockings. I recall that on Xmas Eve, my father called my brother and me to the window and pointed out a flashing red light in the sky, telling us we'd better get to bed because that sure looked like Santa flying in high over Long Island.

Early the next morning we dove into a pile of carefully wrapped gifts: new tricycles and bicycles, sleds, a fringed Davy Crocket shirt, and stockings full of goodies. I don't recall ever being disappointed. Years later, I often wondered how my father, who was totally non-mechanical, was able to assemble toys without them falling apart at the first touch.

My wife and I continued that tradition with our sons. Naturally, being a Christian of sorts, my wife is really into the decorating thing and gift overload. The boys were never disappointed. Setting up bikes, Darth Vader's Death Star Command Post, slot car racetracks, etc., through the night, I was always a bit stressed to meet a deadline, but it was a labor of love.

Naturally the best Christmases then, as now, were the snow-covered ones... white Christmases. With ten inches already on the ground and more on the way, we'll be having a white Christmas with our sons and their better halves this year here in New Hampshire. On Christmas Eve afternoon, we'll go down to the town service station and partake of their annual Xmas party amid the lifts, tires, and oil-absorbing media. Later that evening we'll stop by the neighbors for drinks and finger food.

And in the morning, aside the wood stove, sipping coffee in our jammies, Mrs. Hump and I will relive our own childhoods vicariously through the "kids" as they open their gifts, tease each other, make a mess with the paper, all while the dogs run through it yapping and chewing on their own new toys.

Christmas by any other name is a day of family, if you're lucky enough to have one. It's a time to share drinks and food with friends. To show your appreciation to your loved ones and people who do so much for us throughout the year. And to share what bounty you have with those less fortunate.

For this atheist and his family, it's never been about impossible man-gods, or mythical virgin births, or denying reality. Just the opposite—it's a celebration of family, friends, and snow-covered childhood memories. Nothing is more real than that.

43

What Are Atheists Apologizing For?

22 Dec 2009

Hemant Mehta happens to be one of my favorite atheists. I visit his blog, "The Friendly Atheist," at least once a day religiously (http:// friendlyatheist.com/).

The other day he posted an article about a North Carolina atheist group who won the right to post a sign adjacent to a Christmas display on city property. You can read it here: http://friendlyatheist.com/page/2/, although you'll get the gist of it from this essay.

While most of his readership approved of the sign and commended the organization for its commitment to not acquiesce to this Christian need for implicit governmental endorsement by promoting their beliefs on public property, some of them were less than fully supportive. Here are some of those comments:

- *"… a lot of those ignorant people will react immediately with anger, not curious thoughtfulness, when they see this… I'm still undecided on how I feel about this."*

- *"I like the message on the sign. However, since it mentions 'mythological gods' in reference to Jesus, people will be utterly outraged."*
- *"...it sounds to me as though it's saying, 'No, stupid, Jesus isn't the reason it gets cold in winter— that's because of the axial tilt,' as if religious people are beyond understanding that (when in fact, it's not what religious people are saying anyway). I don't like it at all."*
- *"I think the holiday displays should be inspirational and could do without the lesson."*
- *"[Atheists'] confrontational messages can sometimes come across as being snippy or negative..."*

Yes, some theists will react with anger. Yes, it implies Jesus is just one of many gods man has honored on December 25 and that they are all mythical. Yes, it clearly states Xmas was co-opted from pagan celebrations of the winter solstice. Yes, it could be interpreted as confrontational, and the mindless that intentionally deny history and object to reality may well be offended. So what?

If Christians need to draw "inspiration" from illuminated plastic statues in a publicly owned arena, then their faith is pretty damn weak. I have no obligation to underwrite their inspiration. They can draw their inspiration from plastic religious displays on private property, thank you.

Exactly what are these ambivalent atheists so tentative about? Is documentable truth so painful that it must go on tiptoe so as to avoid bruising the sensibilities of the deluded who demand their religion be given special governmental endorsement by singular placement on public property? Is a believer's potential offense by the secular sign more valued and more worthy of respect and sensitivity than my offense at their religious intrusion on property I pay to support?

Do we really need to worry about appearing "snippy" to theists lest they might think ill of atheists and condemn us as immoral, unethical, godless communists unworthy to hold public office and seeking to destroy the country? Many of them already think that.

Sure, let the apologizing and accommodating atheists wring their hands over possibly offending the willfully ignorant with a truthful statement on the origin of the holiday season. Maybe when the annual Holocaust-denier convention comes around, the same weak-kneed atheists should scorn any attempts to offset the haters' denial and ignorance with truth and reality lest it injure the sensibilities of the anti-Semites and enflame their ire.

I love that atheist group's sign. There should be one wherever religionists seek to use public property to promote their beliefs. No apologies necessary.

44

Loving the One You Fear: The Peculiar Christian Dilemma

27 Dec 2009

Imagine, if you will, being devoted to and in love with someone who has committed mass murder and various atrocities throughout his life. Imagine this individual set up a test for his earliest relatives knowing in advance they would fail and that he would punish their progeny forever. He readily admits he killed his own son and was psychotic enough to demand another man kill his only child as a test of the man's fealty, stopping him only at the very last moment.

Consider that this person created a place of eternal pain and everlasting horror and has the power to commit you there if you don't profess your love for him. Of course he says that you have free will to love him or not, but if you choose "not," he's going to send you to be tortured forever.

He demands that you praise him for these things... regularly; he expects your worship of him and him alone; he wants you to eat his body and drink his blood in exchange for his benevolence.

What if this was your father, or husband, or boyfriend? Could your love be genuine? Could you profess it freely and without intimidation? Would you acquiesce to his demands out of fear? Or would you try to find an out, an escape, a safe house, perhaps seek an order of protection?

The description above sounds like it could be the movie script for the next *Saw* sequel. But it's much worse than a horror film. There are two billion people to whom this being is not some fictional movie fiend but their much-admired and beloved *"Father who art in heaven"* to whom they profess their undying love and devotion. Father!?

Many abused and battered women have so little self-esteem, so little confidence in themselves that they cling to their abuser and genuinely believe they love him. They will say, *"Oh, that was the old him…he's changed now. Besides, it was my own misbehavior that provoked him and made him do these things. He promises me I'll be rewarded eventually. He loves me. It's all good."* But all the while they know the possibility exists that if they slip they will be horribly killed or continuously punished. The unpredictability of this demented thing adds another dimension of horror. It is their fear that cements their "love." It's a terrible fact of reality for some women. Society as a whole abhors and condemns it.

And yet, when that fiend, that bully, that psychopath is the imagined Supreme Being that has been thrust upon them since childhood, society says, *"This is good. How could you not want such a Father? Join me in my love born of fear."*

What a hideous dilemma and existence Christians submit to: indoctrinated to love something by fear of its power and wrath, and let it rule your life even when it doesn't exist. When confronted with this reality, they will deny their fear, even employing words like "God-respecting" to redefine "God-fearing" in gentler terms. But denial and repressing the facts do not change them. To me that sounds like the definition of Hell on Earth.

45

The Obscenity of Christian Apologetics

01 Jan 2010

I stumbled across an apologetics website ironically dubbed *Rational Christianity*. In it the writer sets up challenges to certain biblical passages from hypothetical believers who express their concern for the cruelty of the Bible. He then commences to explain away these horrific acts in a manner that is meant to placate the concerns of the supposed questioning believer (http://www.rationalchristianity.net/genocide.html).

One particular set of questions and answers stunned me. In examining the genocidal destruction of a neighboring tribe by the Israelites, the straw man questioner asks: "*What about the children...why did they in their innocence have to die?*"

Here is the *Rational Christian's* explanation: "*Why were the children killed, if they weren't guilty? Apparently, they were considered as morally neutral, since they weren't yet old enough to be held accountable or to have done much right or wrong. While not as corrupt as their parents, they were part of the society that was judged, and shared its earthly (though not its eternal) fate.... When a person or a society committed massive evil, that evil was punished by the destruction of the entire family or city; in such cases, only those who had actively demonstrated their integrity could be saved..."*

In a nutshell, the children were too young to be guilty or corrupt in the eyes of God. But they were unlucky enough to have been born to parents and into a culture that offended God, so he killed them all. But not to worry: the dead kids get to go to a fun afterlife versus their parents, who will be punished even after death. So it's all good.

This isn't the worst of it. The next question was: *"Couldn't the children have died painlessly? In fact couldn't God have just taken them up to heaven and spared them from physical death?"*

The *Rational Christian* answers: *"Since the children lived in a world affected by sin, they faced its earthly consequences...only a few righteous people were translated into heaven, namely Enoch and Elijah. As noted above, since the children had not shown themselves to be righteous, they were not spared the common fate of death. ... It's worth noting that being killed with a sword (perhaps beheaded) was at the time one of the quickest ways for the children to die as opposed to suffocation/strangulation, starvation, disease or being torn apart by wild animals..."*

So there you have it. If only the infants and toddlers had done something, acted overtly, to demonstrate their righteousness, then God would have spared them. If instead of sucking dumbly at their mothers' breasts and spending their days soiling their diapers, they had just taken it upon themselves to worship the God of Abraham, or kept kosher, or hadn't worn mixed fiber swaddling clothes, or perhaps if they had stoned a homosexual or two to death, then God would have deemed them worthy of being spared the death penalty. But, no...they didn't rise to the occasion. They paid with their short lives.

But not to worry...it's all good! Chopping the head off of a baby, after all, was one of the quickest ways to kill it. Well, that and smashing its head against a stone wall. No muss, no fuss. I mean, isn't it obvious how merciful God was? Heck, he could have sent bears to tear them apart and didn't. (God has done that to children before, but only once and only forty-two of them.)

Note the businesslike, matter-of-fact replies. Note the absence of anything approaching horror, sadness, or wonderment at such callous treatment by a supposedly merciful, loving God. Instead, we get a dispassionate justification for mass infanticide, a strident defense of an indefensible act that would disgust and horrify any normal, thinking, moral human being.

When Herod kills the Jewish infants, it's called "The Slaughter of the Innocents." When their God kills pagan children, it's fully understandable and righteous. Obscene.

I can't help but wonder if people like this actually believe their apologetics. Maybe they are just compelled to defend the faith no matter how grotesque and horrific it may be. That or I underestimated the ability of the religious to delude themselves. Either way, I'm happy I lack that trait.

46

The Open-Minded vs. the Empty-Headed

06 Jan 2010

"*If you just were more open-minded, you would see the truth and let Jesus into your heart.*"
That sentence or its variations is a favorite of proselytizing theists. In essence, they are saying unless you believe like they do, you must be close-minded. Or, more succinctly, open your mind and let your brain fall out.

Open-minded
—adjective
1. having or showing a mind receptive to new ideas or arguments
2. unprejudiced; unbigoted; impartial (http://dictionary.reference.com/browse/openminded)

Given the definition, it is irrational for theists to posit that unless one accepts the religionist's belief once it has been fully explored, evaluated, and discounted that one is not open-minded. Most of us have been exposed to and/or explored religious supernaturalism; those of us who see no logical basis for it, no visible means of support, no evidence of its efficacy reject it. That's not being close-minded; it's being discerning.

It would be akin to telling someone who tasted and disliked an exotic dish that they were "close-minded" for not liking it just because you do. They would only be close-minded had they declared it not to their liking having not first sampled the dish.

The 9/11 and Obama-hating "birther" conspiracy theorists continue to retain their hold on delusion and conspiratorial nonsense in the face of a preponderance of verifiable and testable evidence to the contrary. No amount of evidence that discredits their mindset will ever influence their position. That is close-minded absolutism.

Meanwhile, those of us who have heard their conspiracy rants, have read and evaluated their "proofs" and rejected them as tainted wishful (hateful) thinking, and have examined the independent, overwhelming, genuine evidence for no conspiracy are accused by these nuts of lacking an open mind.

One would lack an open mind if he rejected the conspiracy theories or religious precepts out of hand without having ever examined and explored them. I have examined them. I have explored them. In the case of religion, I have done so in its many different flavors and varied perspectives. And using my powers of reason and ability to weigh evidence, I reject it as superstitious nonsense *unless and until objective evidence of the divine is presented that will supplant evidence to the contrary.* What could be more open-minded than that?

Fundamentalist religious fanatics reject science, typically having never actually read a genuine scientific source document. I'll speculate that not one in twenty-five thousand Creationists have actually read

Darwin's *On the Origin of Species* or Dawkins' *Greatest Show on Earth*. Yet they reject evolutionary theory/natural selection as fallacy. That is *prejudiced*, that is *partisan*, and that is *non-receptivity* to the input of new ideas or argument. That is close-minded. It exists because just to investigate (never mind accept) the voluminous scientifically corroborated evidence for an old Earth and evolution from a vast array of disciplines would undermine their belief. It's a denial reflex. It's the hallmark of the absolutist.

When an Evangelical fundie pulls the old *"if you were more open-minded..."* ploy, tell them which Biblical verse is among the most incredible and unbelievable to you and why. Then ask them which of Darwin's specific detailed observations on the island variants of the Galapagos tortoise in support of natural selection is least credible to them and why. The open-minded will always vanquish the mindless absolutist.

47

Christianity and Morality: By Revelation or Evolution?

11 Jan 2010

Christians will tell you that there is only one divinely revealed religion, and that theirs is it.

A number of religions claim revelation by God. Islam claims Allah revealed his word to Mohammed. Mormons claim that their doctrine was revealed to Joseph Smith by Moroni, and all subsequent LDS doctrinal revisions were revealed to successive church presidents by God. Christians dismiss Islam as simply fiction and its followers as dupes. They deride Mormon claims as nonsense and Mormonism as a cult at best, not even Christian at worst.

But what gives mainstream Christianity's claim of revelation more validity than the Mormon or Muslim claims? What objective evidence can any of them offer? The New Testament, the Qur'an, the Book of Mormon... one a fairytale sequel to a Bronze-Age book of cultist prophesy fulfillment and myth, one the hate-filled misogynistic ranting of a child-molesting warlord, and another the testimony of a convicted charlatan.

If Christianity was revealed and was not a result of religious evolution, how is it that so many pre-Xtian pagan gods share some of the same characteristics and miraculous events as those attributed to Jesus? How is it that so many Christian holidays were co-opted from pagan festivals and observances? Why did the Reformation mutate from Catholicism, giving birth to so many new denominations? And exactly which one of the twenty-eight thousand denominations and sects of Christianity was revealed by God? With their varied rituals and interpretations of God's words, they can't all be revealed else they'd all be in agreement.

The idea of revelation is just another aspect of man-made religious delusion. It's one religion's desire to stake its claim to ownership of the ultimate "Truth." Religious practices have evolved beyond human sacrifice, animal sacrifice, burnt offerings, and temple prostitutes, just as technology has evolved from chariots to airplanes. We see it evolving right before our eyes as the Catholic Church accepts evolutionary theory, and liberal Christians reject biblical inerrancy.

If Judeo-Christian morality was revealed, why did God not reveal his condemnation of slavery in an eleventh commandment? Why didn't Jesus condemn it fifteen hundred years later? Why did it take almost four thousand years of Judeo-Christian morality for Western society to outlaw it? Was its final eradication in Western civilization a matter of divine intervention/ revelation, or the result of man's naturally evolving mortality and ethics?

Judeo-Christian claims of being the moral beacon and holding the ethical high ground has been falsified many times and is hardly well represented in scripture. Morality evolved and continues to evolve today—equal rights for women, gays, and minority races, rejection of genocide, and the gradual elimination of capitol punishment, none of which was sanctioned by the Bible or revealed by a supreme being.

Religion's evolution toward liberalism and reason, and morality's evolution away from the static and bigoted precepts of scriptural declarations are unstoppable, just as evolution of species is unstoppable. Someday the unyielding grasp of religiously interpreted moral dictates will fall to the moral imperatives of a society evolving toward equality and acceptance.

Eventually religion will become extinct as it fails to compete with reason and reality. Much like natural selection, it's simply a matter of survival of the fittest.

48

"Drive a Spike through my hand...I'm Feelin' Christ-like Today"

15 Jan 2010

There's nothing like religion to inspire people to do crazy things that no sane person on the planet would otherwise do.

Many early religions had human sacrifice. It was practiced in proto-Hebraic religions throughout the Middle and Far East, and in Europe by the Druids. In the New World, the Aztecs and Mayans perfected it, making it a high-production spectator sport until the Conquistadors wiped them out in the sixteenth century.

The Egyptian pharaohs and nobles had people, volunteers even, buried alive in their tombs to serve them in the afterlife. Wives of dead Hindu Brahmans threw themselves onto their husband's funeral pyres to join them in the great beyond.

Some American Indian tribes performed the ritual sun dance, which included having barbs pierced through the flesh on one's back and being hoisted up on a scaffold. Some plains tribes shot arrows into a selected virgin, wounding her repeatedly until mercifully putting one through her heart.

Today, Muslims in western India throw babies off of buildings and catch them (usually) in open sheets. Somehow this is supposed to ensure good health. In many Muslim countries they practice *Ashura* bloodletting, where the child's head is cut with a knife and blood allowed to drip down, soaking his clothes as he screams. Naturally, in neither case is the child consulted beforehand.

Of course, the Jews are famous for circumcision of male children on the eighth day after birth. The good news is it's done with a scalpel now, having done away with the earlier flint knife and largely eliminating the use of the elder's teeth.

Christians have some lovely rituals. In the Philippines on Easter, men drag a full-size crucifix across cobblestones until bloodied, and/or they are "scourged," given the old forty lashes, just like Jesus according to the Gospels. Some even volunteer to have nails driven through their palms into a cross and are briefly hung out to dry. The thorn of crowns is an optional accessory.

In fact, Christians have a long history of mortification of the flesh: wearing a hair shirt, self-flagellation with chains or leather thongs with metal on the end, walking on their knees, and the wearing of a *cilice*, a leather or chain band with spikes that cut into the thigh of the voluntary wearer (the albino monk in the *DaVinci Code* wore one).

In the ancient religions, blood-lettings were intended to placate the gods, give victory in war, or bring fertility to the tribe's women and crops. They were ignorant of science, thus their beliefs, rituals, and lives were entirely controlled by shaman and the ruling authority, who were often one in the same.

But modern-day practice of this kind of self-abuse in order to ensure health, mark one's special relationship to a god, or put to death the desires of the flesh is simply barbaric, bordering on insane, and voluntary. For what purpose is this pain and agony inflicted or endured? To show some supernatural sky buddy how much they love him? To be at one with a mythical man-god who may or may not have ever existed and who certainly isn't going to applaud them? To be seen as more devout and devoted to this magical being than their neighbor?

Whatever the reason, it isn't driven by rational thought. It's a product of the religion mind virus that prompts people to behave like pain-inflicting, blood-letting, masochistic cultists. Only the deluded could possibly justify it, much less endure it.

Of course, if crucifying Christian fundies like Pat Robertson and his ilk would bring world peace, end starvation, ensure tolerance and equality for all, drop the price of oil, and help the economy to recover, I'd fully endorse them all doing it on a daily basis. I'd even lend them my nail gun.

49

Militant Atheist: "To Be or Not to Be?" That Is the Question

20 Jan 2010

I place myself in the Hitchens, Harris, PZ Meyers school of aggressive anti-theist militant atheism. If not for people like them, and organizations that share their tack, we would not be seeing the surge in rational thought and outspoken opposition coming from previously closeted atheists and agnostics who are now "coming out."

The contributions of scientists, the best of whom are non-believers of varying degrees, whose efforts have led to medical advances, longer life spans for humanity, technology that just a hundred years ago was unimagined are rarely if ever praised by the religionists. They see science as the bulwark of anti-religious thought. So much for atheists gaining legitimacy in the eyes of religionists with their gentility, reason, and contributions to society. Theists will credit God instead.

Some say that engaging in aggressive reasoned debate will never change the mind of those who are absolutists, who base their lives on supernaturalism to which they were exposed at an early age. I agree. It is just as unlikely to yield fruit as religious proselytizing will cause a thinking person to suddenly abandon reason for supernaturalist belief. But what debate does do is give fence-sitters something to think about, chew on. If they are prompted to question the unquestionable precepts of faith, something religions do not encourage, then by observing a realist in aggressive debate, their curiosity may be piqued and their reasoning skills along with it.

Those who despise atheists, distrust them, see them as immoral and un-American will not be swayed by a kinder, gentler approach—my reference to scientists is one example. The fundamentalist theist, be it Christian or Muslim, are as firm in their dismissal of science and atheists as they are immersed in their supernaturalist beliefs. We'd be deceiving ourselves to think otherwise. The women's suffrage movement didn't win the right to vote by being kinder and gentler. Nor did blacks attain civil rights by just being good citizens and walking on tiptoe to the back of the bus. Nor did the gay rights movement win any converts to full equality and tolerance by working in soup kitchens or contributing to the Salvation Army.

Every one of those movements realized that the kinder and gentler method of whispering their desire for equality was perceived as weakness, powerlessness, and impotence by the majority opposition. A strong front challenging the religious right, demanding that the Separation of Church and State be kept sacrosanct, fighting theist intrusions into our lives, schools, and government, calling out the fakes, frauds, and exposing the unbalanced words and deeds of religionists is how we will gain influence and retain our freedom. If they take offense, so what?

Islam continues to flood into Western society. With some governments' and the media's failure to stand firm against Muslim threats of violence if demands for the limitation of free speech where their religion is concerned isn't observed, we are reinforcing their perception of us as the spineless *"infidels."* If the West doesn't pull its head out of the sand and change its approach, Islamic Fundamentalists will continue to capitalize on it, the virus will spread, and Western culture will continue contributing to its own eventual demise.

So if we are militant as atheists, if we push it to the wall and go toe to toe with theist ignorance, arrogance, and intolerance, what's the worst that can happen? Muslims will riot, burn, and threaten us with domination and death? They already do that. Christians will hate us, mistrust us, and deny our patriotism and morality? They already do that, too. We need to make it crystal-clear that as freethinkers we are not doormats to mindless fanaticism; that the days of pretending to be theist are over, that expectations of respect for their archaic beliefs can be forgotten, and that we won't give an inch to their attempts at creeping theocracy. There will be no appeasement, no compromise, no negotiating with ancient delusion.

I'm a militant atheist. I could be nothing else.

50

"Stop Reading Anti-Religion Books!" A Religionist's Appeal for Tolerance of the Intolerable

30 Jan 2010

L ast week I finally got around to posting a five-star review on amazon.com for Dr. Darrel Ray's *The God Virus*. It's an outstanding and unique perspective of how religion infects all our lives, promulgates, and negatively impacts civilization.

One of the very few negative reviews for the book was posted by someone who declares herself to be neither an atheist nor a Christian. Besides her simplistic dismissal of science as "arrogant," and a complete misunderstanding of the term "God virus," there was this gem:

"Let's have some more tolerance here. You should not need to constantly read books about how bad religion is if you are secure about who you are. You should not need this validation."

My reply to her fallacious comment follows:

Tolerance? As in the tolerance carriers of the fundamentalist God Virus have for homosexuals' equal rights and happiness?

You mean like the tolerance extremist anti-abortionists have for OBGYNs who perform legal procedure but are killed for it, or their offices bombed? Or the tolerance that would disallow women control of their own bodies? Or that seeks to force raped women to bare her rapist's child?

You mean like the tolerance Catholics have for condom use while HIV runs rampant in Third World countries, killing millions?

Perhaps you mean the tolerance religionists have for the scientific reality of global warming and the scientists who seek to stem it, while they turn a blind eye to it or deny it because "Jesus is coming anyway"?

Tolerance such as Muslims have for apostates from Islam, or Jews, or for "infidels"—"truths" with which they infect each succeeding generation?

Tolerance Islam has for free speech when that speech is deemed offensive to their inane belief?

We should have tolerance for using a god as justification for "crusades" against nations that did us no harm?

Tolerance for theistically inspired revisionist history?

We should tolerate those who want to set back the teaching of science in our classrooms three hundred years?

We should tolerate obstacles to better health, and simply accept devastating illnesses or crippling injuries by opposing research like religious extremists do because it supposedly offends their imaginary God?

We should tolerate those who want to transform the USA into a "Christian Nation," a theocracy?

Don't talk to me about having tolerance for those religionists whose worldview is driven and controlled by a book that itself endorses hideous acts of immorality that is rife with the lies, delusions, and thirst for control of an ancient patriarchal society whose infamous intolerance toward the beliefs of others was manifested by barbaric laws, tribal genocide, and enslavement.

Reading books about the dangers inherent in radical fundamentalist religion, how it negatively impacts our lives and threatens our culture, isn't about how "secure" one is in their non-belief. It's about opening doors to understanding how supernaturalism in its most virulent and even more benign forms impacts us for the worse as a civilization and on an individual basis.

That you don't get it speaks to your own strain of religious mind virus. That you condemn reading such books is a manifestation of that illness.

51

On the Bible, Disgust, and Revulsion

11 Feb 2010

I've read the KJV and NIV Bible from end to end. It's remarkable that so many people who claim to have read the Bible can still retain any reverence for it, give it credibility, and not be disgusted and repelled by it. Perhaps the answer lies in the selectivity of which books of the Bible they read and which they ignore. Perhaps they prefer instead to see a kindly Magician-Man-God that performs miraculous tricks and shows a kinder, gentler, post anger-management therapy persona while still retaining the ability to wantonly kill pigs, destroy fig trees, and steal donkeys.

In voicing this opinion, I was taken to task by a fellow atheist:

"There's no point in being disgusted/repelled by the Bible. It portrays how we were more than two thousand years ago. The vengeful Old Testament God is how the primitive people of this time period would have imagined their deity.

"Similarly, you can read The Iliad *and observe how war and superstition were so predominant in the Greek world.*

Both The Iliad *and the stories of the Bible were invented in an attempt to find meaning in a cruel, violent world."*

And he would be correct if the Bible were read by everyone as simply a reflection of an earlier civilization's thought processes and justifications for their barbarism. Then indeed the horrific acts can be viewed in the context of the times. Nothing more need be said.

But that is far from the case with the Bible. The events depicted are attributed to a God who is still worshipped to this day. That God is credited in this scripture with establishing rules and instigating behaviors that, by any reasonable interpretation, are cruel, immoral, and counter-productive to human development.

The Bible is myth accepted as truth. Millions assign it divine authority by a God that is still worshipped and it is held in reverence in spite of the horrific wonton acts it is credited with inspiring. These acts should be abhorrent to anyone with an objective perspective of humanity and morality, but instead they are excused, apologized, rationalized, and justified by its adherents. *That* is what makes it repellent and disgusting, and that is what separates it from any other ancient myth narrative.

No one still worships Moloch, the pagan god who demanded live infant incineration. I'm unaware of anyone who worships the Greek pagan gods that chained men to rocks and sent birds of prey to eat their livers for eternity, or the gods of the Aztecs and Mayans that thirsted for massive quantities of human blood. If they still did, and if there were scripture for those religions, and if the modern-day adherents praised those gods and that scripture and declared them good and just and worthy of respect, I dare say every atheist and every follower of the Abrahamic religions would be unanimous in their revulsion and disgust for those religions' scriptures as well. "Obscene" would not be too strong a description.

If there is "no point" in being disgusted and repelled by a book that glorifies genocide and injustice, yet is still revered today, then there is no point in being disgusted by the words of Fred Phelps and those who hold him in esteem. Besides, there doesn't have to be a point. Reviling hate, oppression, injustice, and barbarism should be the natural response of a civilized people.

52

Those Damn Arrogant Atheists!

24 Feb 2010

I recently joined a new Facebook page entitled *"Atheism—we believe in ourselves."* I don't join every atheist group or page suggested to me, but I like to give support to Facebook friends who start a page. I also am not crazy about the use of the word "believe" in the name, but I won't push the point.

One member of the group posted this: *"It's self-centered and unenlightened to say one believes in oneself."*

I found this a rather peculiar comment coming from a self-proclaimed atheist. What? Is it more enlightened to believe in a Sky Buddy who manipulates your life and promises you eternal existence after death? If not, what's the alternative to belief in oneself (aka, confidence in one's self, self-reliance): dependence on others to manage your life for you? People who do not believe in themselves lack self-esteem, lack independence, lack self-reliance, never take risks that could advance their career or give them a competitive advantage in any life endeavor.

In discussing this in another atheist forum, one member said this: "...*announcing to believers [in his very Catholic country, the Philippines] that one believes in oneself as opposed to an invisible being in the sky simply comes across as putting one's self over God. It is therefore to be expected that (some) believers will find it arrogant and self-centered...*"

Do we not put ourselves over all imaginary beings? I know I do. Do we need to be ashamed of that? I'm not; in fact I couldn't be more proud of it. And if theists find us arrogant in our acceptance of reality over superstition and open dismissal of their delusion, do we need to concern ourselves about it? I could understand that being the case fifty or one hundred years ago or during the Spanish Inquisition, but not now. Not anymore.

I'm unconcerned about bruising the sensibilities of those who prefer we remain contrite in our acceptance of reality and reason, or that we remain invisible to the theist majority. We must embrace confrontation. If it wasn't for Madalyn Murray O'Hair, Ingersoll, Dawkins, Hitchens, Dennett, Harris, and others who have kicked wide the door and said, "Enough!" to false respect for theist beliefs, to religious dominance, to salving theists' fragile sensibilities, we'd all be pretending to be believers. I doubt I could even openly write this piece, or this book.

The degree of religiosity in the Philippines, I dare say, is no worse than the degree of religiosity in certain parts of the US. Mississippi is the most religious state in the union with 96 percent believers, according to the Pew Forum survey. Yet there are a number of groups down there who openly declare their atheism, challenge fundamentalist intrusions across the line of church/state separation, and are quite vocal. Yep, they are probably perceived as arrogant by their believing neighbors, especially given their more advanced "*book larnin*" and godless rationality. Good!

Yes, I put myself over gods, all of them. Yes, I have complete confidence in my ability to manage my life without incorporeal nonsense. No, I won't hide my rejection of belief in a closet or fret over my presumed "arrogance" that is born of self-confidence, education, self-reliance, and respect for reality. Besides, what's more arrogant than the ignorance of faith in the great "Truth" to which each religion stakes claim?

If my "in-your-face" demeanor causes religionists angst, too bad. If it incites them to something more, bring it on.

53

Application for God Status: Résumé Attached

01 Mar 2010

Over coffee this morning, I was thinking that I have all the necessary qualifications to establish my own divinity, even have people pray to me and worship me. So I have been pulling my résumé together. Here's what I have so far:

June 2007: My eldest son and his wife disobeyed me when I told them not to touch my bowl of dried banana chips. I threw them out of the house, banished them back to New York, and told them that they and their yet unborn offspring are cursed for life. They didn't take it well.

September 2007: I decided I didn't like the way things were going in my town. I blew up the dam upstream, which flooded the entire region, killing every man, woman, child, and animal in the county except for my friend Gary, his wife and son, and their three Boston terriers. They're the only folks I liked.

January 2008: I convinced this mentally challenged guy that unless he killed his own son with an axe, I was going to heap some bad mojo on him. He was just about to lower the boom on the kid when I stopped him at the last second. I was just testing him. He may have soiled his pants. I know his kid did. It was a hoot.

March 2008: My followers and friends clearly were in need of some easy-to-remember rules, so I came up with my "Top Ten List of Stuff Hump Wants You to Do." I made sure the first four rules were all about me. Hey, I have a fragile ego.

May 2008 - August 2008: Lots of little things were irking me during this period. Maybe it was the heat, maybe I was just cranky, I dunno.

Things like folks wearing their damn mixed poly-ester/cotton blend clothes, people eating lobster without lemon, farmers cross-breeding cattle to get more milk production, men giving other men hand jobs (same with women)— hundreds of other things like that which perturbed me for no particular rhyme or reason.

So I decided those things are illegal around here. I've directed my followers to kill those who do this stuff. I posted the following sign on my neighbor's cornfield: "*No Gleaning Fields on Thursdays before 8:00 a.m. and after 3:00 p.m. during Baseball Season if You Value Your Life, Damnit!*" My neighbor asked what this was all about since it made no sense. I had him and his family smited.

November 2008: This big extended family down the road didn't think much of me and my followers. They practiced some strange ways, ya know? I think they are Asians, probably pagans. Some of them actually ate lobster salad without mayo on *hamburger buns*!! Disgusting!!

So I told my friends and followers to set their house on fire and kill every one of them—their dogs, cats, and farm animals, too! I told them it's okay to make an exception for the little girls. Hey, some of my friends like 'em young. I tried to get them to wipe out the town of Bellows Falls, just across the border in Vermont, but the town's two cops had those aluminum meter maid electric carts, so they were too powerful for us.

March 2009: I decided to have another son. Mrs. Hump became hysterical at the idea and threatened me with a knife. I had no idea how to find myself a wife of child-bearing age on short notice—and my inflatable Mary doll wasn't in any position to reproduce. So I snuck up on some stoner chick, gave her some Ruffies, and nailed her. She never knew what happened. Late in December, she gave birth to our son. She figured it was a virgin birth. Hey...I wasn't about to confess to anything, so I let her think that.

January 2010: I was thinking my new bastard son was gay. I wasn't sure, but he was spending all his free time with this group of a dozen or so effeminate guys with long hair and playing his X-box. (I'll admit he has remarkable control of that thing for a thirteen-month-old. Pretty damn miraculous! A chip off the old block in that respect.)

So to make him prove his manhood I told him to get himself all worked up and pissed off, and go inject the neighbor's goats with anti-freeze and have them jump off a cliff. He did and they did. Then, to have him prove he's no panty-waist tree-hugger, I told him to kill a pear tree for not having pears on it. He babbled something at first about my being an idiot because there are no trees bearing fruit in January in New Hampshire. But he killed the tree anyway. He's a good boy, albeit a bit of a smart-ass and given to hissy fits, though.

Spring 2010: I plan to have my little bastard son tortured to death to demonstrate to the town's folk what a compassionate and caring guy I am to my followers. No doubt he'll get a little rattled toward the end, but he's a skinny kid and probably won't last too long...three or four hours max. He's resilient, though, so who knows? A couple of defibrillator shocks and he might come back. *"CLEAR!!"*

Now, these are just some of the highlights. I have a lot more stuff to fill in, more detail. You know, pad my deity qualifications a bit. But I think I've got something going here. After all, how could anyone not worship a guy like that?

54

Welcome to Capitulation to Creeping Theism 101

05 Mar 2010

Good morning class, I'm Professor Hump. For the next three minutes I will be your instructor. Many of you have seen me on campus and know me to be an ardent atheist activist. But not today, not for this class. Today I will lead you on a field trip through the wonderful world of atheist accommodation in the early twenty-first century.

Let's begin by reading this news article about a man in Mississippi who demanded that the crosses carved into the courthouse pews that were salvaged from a church be removed. The Xtian mayor of the town plans to fight him tooth and nail. No woosie *that* Xtian redneck, no siree. The story can be found here: http://www.myeyewitnessnews.com/news/local/story/ Olive-Branch-Man-Says-Church-Pews-in-Court-are/QXj-qP-7-0GFC1n2cewC3Q.cspx.

You can bet your student loans that if those pews had a Star of David carved into them instead of a cross, the good mayor wouldn't have accepted them even for free. If they had a Wicca symbol, he'd likely have had them burned.

Now, let us examine some of the responses to this story posted by some alleged atheists to Hemant Mehta's *Friendly Atheist* blog.

Atheist A: *"This guy needs to be a friendlier atheist."*

I bet many of you think that no religious symbols belong as a fixture in any courtroom in this country, in any way, for any reason. Evidently you're mistaken, as evidenced by Atheist A, who would prefer to just roll over and be a "friendlier atheist." Thank you, Mr. Step-and-Fetch-It.

Atheist B: *"If the pews are functional ignore the crosses. You can be strong enough not to be offended by the trivial."*

I know just what he means. I feel the same way about the inclusion of intelligent design/creationism in public school science books, or a giant cross erected on public land, or biblical verses emblazoned on military rifle sights by the manufacturer, or a Muslim crescent hung on the wall of the local Motor Vehicle Bureau, etc. If the books, rifle sights, parks, and government offices are functional, we can just ignore those chapters, ignore those verses, ignore those symbols; we are strong enough not to be offended by the "trivial." Thank you, Mr. Neville Chamberlain-of-Non-Believers.

That concludes today's introduction to Capitulation to Creeping Theism 101. Tomorrow we will open with an invocation delivered by a fundamentalist Evangelical pastor. Yes, I know this is a publicly funded college and we are atheists, but, hey, he insisted, so let's just be nice.

Your homework assignment is to find more ways to set back secularists' hard-won advancements by fifty years. Class dismissed.

55

The Eternal Question That Proves God—But Only for the Deluded

10 Mar 2010

"*W*hy is there something rather than nothing?" "What is your explanation for why we exist?"

This tired Christian challenge as an apologetic for the existence of God is frankly unworthy of serious discourse. It is at least one thousand years old, and has been posed and answered many times by philosophers and scientists without having to resort to the supernatural for explanation. And yet the logic of those answers goes in one ear of the theistically impaired and out the other without even slowing down in between. To them the question is, in and of itself, evidence of a god.

Now, don't misunderstand. As a philosophical question, or as a question that helps explain quantum physics, it's useful for mental exercise, discourse, and understanding. It's the religious implication, the theist co-opting of the question for an apologetic agenda to which I object.

Religionists who use this tack don't want the scientific/ rational answers. They've already been tendered; they abound on the Internet and in books brimming with secular reasoning. Theists simply want to continue to repeat the question as a justification for their *"God did it"* explanation for existence, which is their explanation for everything. They like to use it as though it were some esoteric, mystical mind-twister that can only be solved by injecting the supernatural.

It's tantamount to the old *"If evolution is true, and man came from monkeys, how come there are still monkeys?"* That answer, as simple and as obvious as it is to people who understand evolution, natural selection, random mutation, etc., and as often as it has been explained to the unthinking creationists, continues to be ignored by them. The question will be asked ad nauseam no matter how many times the gross ignorance it displays has been soundly and completely dispelled. They will continue to believe that is a chink in evolutionary theory's validity, when all it does is make creationists look vapid.

So, following Occam's razor, which states the best answer is the simplest one, the answer to the Christians' questions of "Why is there something rather than nothing? What is your explanation for why we exist?" is this:

A) Because natural phenomena happen, and they happen to create life when the proper circumstances randomly occur.

B) We exist for the same reason that life likely exists on a multitude of planets in the universe; refer to "A" above.

And as a default answer:

C) There is something rather than nothing because if there were nothing, you couldn't pose your insipid and hackneyed question.

56

Sex, Scandal, and the Impotence of the Catholic Hierarchy

19 Mar 2010

It seems good Pope Benedict is implicated in a cover-up of a child-molesting German priest back in the '80s. Instead of turning him into the authorities, the pope directed him to get psychiatric counseling...all the while the priest continued on with his sexual predilections, being reassigned to another parish, where his perversity continued.

Meanwhile, bishops are under fire as their cover-ups are exposed. All over the planet—Latin America, Ireland, UK, Germany, Austria, France, Poland, Australia, and Canada—victims are coming forward, attesting to decades of priestly sexual abuse. The cover-ups and denials of the Church hierarchy in those countries indicate they don't have a much better track record than the pope or US Church officials. So much for the hackneyed whine of the defensive devout that molesting priests are just a tiny, insignificant minority. That duck doesn't quack anymore.

Oh, sure, the Church will shed crocodile tears. The pope condemns sexual misconduct and I'm sure he'd wish it would all just go away. Some Church officials are admitting they just weren't aggressive enough; they didn't realize the breadth of the problem or its lifelong implications to the victims.

And why should they? These aren't psychologists. They aren't usually trained psychotherapists, sex therapists, social workers, or Special Victims Unit detectives. They are largely sexually repressed shamans who have been trained to read Latin, promote the Church to attract new recruits, accept the impossible as real, and reject the real as impossible. They are wannabe apostles to a myth, dressed in gender-neutral opulent costumes, conducting foolish rituals, embracing magical liturgy, promising nonsensical rewards for belief, forgiving people for sins so they can clean their slates and repeat the sin, and mumbling the same old prayers that fall only on the ears of their awed and cowed parishioners.

It is to these self-imposed eunuchs, these socially impotent pretenders that responsibility rests for ferreting out perverts among their ranks. All the while a goodly number of their own highly placed brethren are themselves doing exactly the same unholy acts. It's the quintessential example of the inmates policing the asylum.

If the Church really understood the depth of the problem, if it cared as much about the victims' well-being as it does about its own financial stability, if it were genuinely invested in rooting out and resolving the problem and ending it once and for all, it would have taken draconian steps to fix it years ago. The pope could have appointed his own VBSMI (Vatican

Bureau of Sexual Misconduct Investigation) with all the power and independence that the Church gave to Tomas de Torquemada, the fifteenth-century leader of the Spanish Inquisition.

When it came to rooting out and punishing imagined enemies of the Church—heretics and back-sliding converted Jews—Torquemada was all-powerful and remarkably effective. But then, those were the good old days when the Church felt threatened by those innocents they considered ungodly. Now that it's the "godly" themselves that threaten the innocents, the motivation isn't quite as strong. They don't want to hear the ugly truth, much less uncover any more of it than absolutely necessary.

It took three hundred and fifty years for the Catholic Church to apologize for the persecution of Galileo, seven hundred and fifty years to apologize for the Inquisition. I'm going to guess that the thousands and thousands of victims of wholesale sexual abuse and cover-up by the Catholic clergy should get their apology in, oh…2500 CE. This assumes the Church doesn't copulate itself into oblivion between now and then.

57

Thanking God

23 Mar 2010

"*I just thank the Lord that he shielded me when all of this took place.*"

This statement was made by one of the guards who were shot by a right-wing fanatic attempting to gain access to the Pentagon a few weeks ago. Both guards' wounds were, fortunately, only superficial.

These kinds of devotional statements seem to fall from believers' mouths faster than M&Ms can fall through the holes in Jesus' hands. Whether it's a crisis from which one escapes serious harm, a victory in a sporting event, winning an election, the remission of a loved one's cancer, or even when fate and probability deal a hideous hand, all reasoned thinking comes to a halt as the believer's brain goes into supernatural mode.

At the National Republican Convention in 2004, Rudy Giuliani said: "*Thank God George Bush is our president.*"

Drew Brees wins the Super Bowl and the first thing out of his mouth to AP is: *"God is great."*

A Canadian survivor of the Haitian earthquake said: *"...thank God for saving my life...praise him for his greatness."*

On a Christian apologetics site, the father of a horribly deformed and vegetative baby offered: *"God blessed us through* [him] *and* [has] *shown Himself to be more real."*

Can these people's logic be any more convoluted, delusional, twisted, and downright obscene?

Fact: 80 percent of gunshot wounds are non-fatal. God or no, the odds were substantially in the guard's favor (http://www.nytimes.com/2008/04/03/nyregion/03shot.html).

Fact: if George Bush had not been elected president, over forty-three hundred US servicemen and -women who have so far died in Iraq would be alive today. If God is responsible for G.W. Bush's presidency, does that mean God is responsible for their needless deaths?

Fact: if "God is great" and his greatness is demonstrated by the New Orleans Saints' victory, it follows that if the Colts had won, God wouldn't be great. Or perhaps he'd be great but only to the Colts fans and not to the Saints fans.

Fact: if God is to be credited for intervening to save a specific individual's life during a natural disaster, then logic has it that God must be blamed for the deaths of over two hundred thousand Haitian earthquake victims not worthy of his mercy.

Fact: if having a deformed, vegetative baby is God's blessing on the parents, the inference is that normalcy would have been a curse or punishment. Worse, it implies the baby's tortured condition is a good thing for him versus normalcy or his parents failing to conceive.

In short, these knee-jerk statements of praise and thanks make no sense from any perspective if one takes a moment to evaluate their meaning. They are senseless not just because there is no God, or because the events/outcomes are all man-made or natural, or because they are a product of probability. They are senseless because the devout perceive their God's action only from their personal perspectives. They don't take a moment to evaluate their God's actions on the broader scale for which he/it is due blame and condemnation, and which is evidence of the fallacy of a loving God.

All of this is lost on theists, of course. Their bleating will go on. Most of them are so far gone that they haven't figured out that the phrase "Thank God it's Friday!" is rather superfluous since Friday happens every seven days…God or no God.

58

Debating YEC: Is There Any
Greater Waste of Intellectual Energy?

28 Mar 2010

I was surfing websites and blogs and came across a two-page war of the words between three or four atheists and a Young Earth Creationist. The subject was "Putting to Rest the Young Earth Creationism Theory."

As I leafed through the twenty-five or so posts, two things became evident:

1. The atheists were presenting reason and science-based discovery that has evolved and improved over a long period of time right up to the most recent scientific evidence for Old Earth.
2. The YEC fundie was repeating the same scripture that hasn't changed in over thirty-five hundred years as his evidence, and repeatedly tried to use pseudo-science to debunk real science.

There were perhaps sixteen or seventeen posts by freethinking scientific types in this thread debunking the foolishness of the YEC myth. My mind boggled at the amount of detail, research, references, links, et al. It caused me to wonder if anyone would put the same amount of effort into debunking things such as:

- Flat Earthers?
- The validity of witchcraft, sorcery, fortune-telling, or magic?
- Alien abduction stories?
- The creation stories of American Indians, Hindus, or any of hundreds/thousands of other such tales?
- Any of the mythical monsters such as Nessy, Champy, Bigfoot, Chupacabra, Yeti?
- Demonic possession?
- Astral projection?
- Transubstantiation?

If the answer is "no" then I can only wonder why this one particular myth, which owes its start to the superstitions and inventiveness of pre-scientific ancients and is dismissed by every credible scientist on the planet, is worthy of such attention. Science has demonstrated through the corroboration and cumulative data of multiple scientific disciplines that the big bang (or a similar event) and evolutionary theory are the cause of the universe and origin of species.

There is as much objective evidence for YEC as there is for aliens building Stonehenge or the pyramids. If scripture alone is their evidence for YEC, there are many more volumes proffering the "theory" of space aliens' influence on the development of human civilization. What imbues one with more credibility than the others? The fact that the OT is pre-scientific age, while these nutty modern-day alien proponents' books are post-scientific age, gives the Bible even less credibility.

Hell, just by calling YEC a "theory," the well-intentioned and time-rich freethinkers have given it more credence than it is due. What next—"Transubstantiation *Theory*"? "Woman into Pillar of Salt *Theory*"? Will arguing against them change anything? Urinating into the wind would be more productive.

This isn't to suggest that Young Earth Creationism or its hybrid but equally vapid brother, Intelligent Design, should get a free pass. Efforts to elevate them as science and put them alongside evolutionary theory in the classroom must be and is being vigorously opposed. Our time and energy are best spent on vigilance of and involvement with local school boards, while our financial support should be given to those watchdog organizations who are on the front line of that battle.

59

Letter to Recovered Theists

05 Apr 2010

I received an email from an Internet friend and activist atheist compatriot. In his letter, he mentioned that he had been too embarrassed to admit to me that he was once the kind of Xtian who advocated biblical inerrancy, including Creationism, defending it against all scientific proofs and reason.

It prompted me to share with him something I've often thought about recovered religious fundamentalists. My letter to him follows. If any of my readers are recovering/recovered fundamentalist theists, this letter is to you as well.

Dear J,

You have nothing to be embarrassed about. You have nothing to be ashamed of. Those who perpetrated the lie, who cultivated it, who fed it to the unwary and who are unrepentant of their scam—those are the ones who should be ashamed and embarrassed.

You were a victim of religious think from childhood to early adulthood. In fact, while your letter compliments me for my reasoned activism, you have more to be proud of about your acceptance of reality than do I. You see, I never had to overcome what you did. I was never indoctrinated, never bombarded with lies and myth at an early age and through my developing years. Thus, I had a head start while you were handicapped.

That you were able to escape from the darkness of unquestioning faith in fable and overcome your handicap speaks to your courage, strength of character, and intellect. I've often wondered had I been in your place, if I would have had the necessary attributes to escape the bonds of religious ignorance and find the door to reason on my own.

As freethinkers we are all "Apostles of Reason." But people like you who overcame what so many others never will are—to borrow a verse from the Bible—among "the most beloved of the apostles." For that you deserve and have my respect, and the respect of every freethinker.

Yours in reason...

60

The Efficacy of Debate and Atheist Proselytizing

11 Apr 2010

> **"...** to use arrogant, derogatory language is counter productive to my motive for engaging [theists] in the first place. ...if your goal in discoursing with theists is to get them to shut up and retreat in awe of your debate skills then, Hump, you have succeeded"—D.

The above is an extract from a letter from a well-meaning atheist of the kinder, gentler persuasion. He took umbrage with my failing to entertain a religious extremist's descent into religious babble in the course of debate, and my bluntness in his dismissal. "D's" motive in engaging theists is to bring them to value the inherent truth in secular thought. A noble enterprise and one that I endorse, but only with those whose level of receptivity and intellect makes them candidates for deprogramming. I do not tolerate fools graciously. I am unrepentant in that regard.

This may not be apparent to certain freethinkers who erroneously assume all levels of believers are receptive to logic and will come around if only one is patient, genteel, reasoned, and avuncular. A couple of decades of atheist activism have taught me otherwise. The rationale is as faulty as a fundie trying to proselytize Richard Dawkins and expecting the desired outcome.

My response to this well-meaning gentleman's chastisement follows.

Dear D,

Most discourse I have with theists is civil and dispassionate. More often than not they are liberal/moderate theists who have some level of receptivity to reality, social justice, and science, and have adjusted their preferred supernatural beliefs to accommodate it. They are receptive to the "truths" of reality. However, that rarely makes for good blog or book fodder.

My "take no prisoner" method is reserved for those theists whose concepts are often dangerous to society and/or patently moronic. These are the fundamentalists and those Christians who do not take the time to explore secular reality/science but reject it out of hand as being a threat to their belief system, who typically resort to absurdities, hackneyed platitudes, defunct apologetics, perversion of scripture and distortion of scientific theory to feed their agenda.

These people are not candidates for "sparking interest in choosing to value truth," as you so eloquently put it. These are people to whom "truth" (i.e., reality/reason) is the enemy, albeit they are unable to perceive that through the fog of their delusion. They are due no respect, they are owed no platform, and their arguments are unworthy of the time or effort of any thinking person. If you believe that the likes of Kirk Cameron, Ray Comfort, Ted Haggard, Pat Robertson, Fred Phelps, or those Christian fanatics, haters, history revisionists, and reality deniers who hold those religious icons in reverence are sub-

ject to being reasoned with, you are operating under a delusion of your own abilities.

I'll waste not a moment trying to throw pearls before swine, anymore than I would spend hours trying to explain the virtue of medical science to a religious fanatic mother who opts to pray over her sick child and allow him to die from an easily curable disease. I'd bitch-slap her and take the kid to the hospital. Period.

I don't toy with them or fool myself into thinking that I am some guiding light and they are receptors of my sage argument and intellect. Those people deserve nothing more than dismissal and utter rejection of their buffoonery. My perspective is the same as Thomas Paine's when he said: "To argue with a man who has renounced his reason is like giving medicine to the dead."

I wish you the best in your endeavor.

61

Interview with an End-Times Prophesying Preacher

17 Apr 2010

The Right Reverend Jeremiah "Billy Bob" Mountebank is the founder and pastor of *The First Fundamentalist Church of Eternal Life and Small Engine Repair* in Picayune, Mississippi. He has caused a stir among his congregation and the press by predicting that the biblical End Times are about to take place. He bases this on scripture and recent worldwide natural disasters—"acts of God," if you will.

On a recent visit to an offshoot congregation in New Hampshire, I had the opportunity to meet with Reverend Mountebank and get the lowdown on the imminent destruction of the world as we know it.

Hump: Reverend Mountebank, I understand you have proclaimed that the End Times are at hand. Since the Bible says no man knows the timing, on what do you base your prediction?

Rev. Mountebank: Please, call me Reverend Billy Bob, there's no point in being formal now with the End at hand.

Hump: Okay, then, Billy Bob.

Rev. BB: That's REVEREND Billy Bob.

Hump: Oh, sorry…Reverend Billy Bob.

Rev. BB: Well, the signs are very clear—tsunamis, meteorites flaming in the sky, earthquakes in Haiti, China, Utah, Chili, mudslides in Brazil, a volcano in Iceland, war and civil unrest in the Holy Land, locust plague in Australia, homos getting married, a nigra president…

Hump [interrupting]: Wait a second, Reverend, what do laws permitting gays to marry or the election of an African-American President have to do with biblical End Times prophesy?

Rev. BB: Well, son, you see it's all part of the sign, you know…natural disasters, chaos, and Satan's growing influence and power affecting the world. Never in the six-thousand-year history of the planet have there been so many disasters, wars, and certainly never homo marriage or nigra world leader.

Hump: But lots of social changes have taken place over the centuries that we now accept as the norm. And natural disasters have been happening every day all over the planet forever: as many as twenty thousand earthquakes a year, fifty a day. It's only that with improvement in communication… the Internet and all…we are made aware of those that happen in populated areas, such as the most recent ones. Besides, earthquakes have only been systematically measured and recorded by scientists for the past hundred years or so out of Earth's 4.6-billion-year history. Volcanoes erupt continuously on land and under water; and as far as war, there has never been a single year in recorded history where war hasn't…

Rev. BB: You've been deceived by Satan, boy!! The Devil has got you to thinking too much. There used to be maybe a dozen or so earthquakes a century, now it's killer earthquakes every week and balls of flame in the sky and hellfire volcanoes in otherwise ice-cold places. It's God telling us to gird our loins an' git ready to come home. Satan is stirring the pot using heathen A-rabs to do his dirty work. He's bending people's minds to accept sodomites as normal folk, causing them Mexicans to swarm over the border, and putting a communist bearer of the mark of Cain, an Afro-Negro or whatever you call them, in charge of Jesus' chosen nation...it's all as the Bible said it would be. Hallelujah!!

Hump: But I've read the Bible and it doesn't mention any-thing about gays, Mexicans, or Black presidents foretelling the End Times.

Rev. BB: CONTEXT, BOY!! CONTEXT!! You got to read the Bible in its proper CONTEXT...it's all there. Besides, God spoke to me and told me the End is near. We was having a bowl of grits and fat back and... Hey! You ain't one of them Liberal Jeeews, or idol-wor-shipping papists, or faggots yer self, are ya? Are you right with the Lord? Are you prepared to meet your maker, welcome the Lord Jesus Christ's return and be embraced by his love, light, kindness, forgiveness, tol-erance, and goodness? Are you saved, boy?

Hump: Actually, I'm an atheist.

Rev. BB: Atheist?? There ain't no such thing—you just hate God and the Baby Jesus, you godless, heathen monkey-worshipper! I'll enjoy watching you burn in hell for an eternity while I'm sipping a cool libation in heaven and stroking the Lord's hair, boy. Now get the hell out of my face, you baby-eating-communist-spawn-of-Satan; there's a Fox camera crew over there and I know THEY love them some Jesus.

62

Observations and Speculation on the Pathology of the Hyper-Religious

29 Apr 2010

I'm not a psychologist...I only play one on the Internet. But I do have a BA in psychology with a minor in religion, a half-century-plus of life experience, and many years of firsthand observations and interactions with the profoundly religiously afflicted.

In my previous book, I discussed hyper-religiosity, a clinical term describing the overt behaviors of certain people suffering from schizophrenia. I also referenced studies that point to childhood sexual abuse by a relative as a cause of high degrees of religiosity in adulthood. Just last week, a passenger on an airplane paraphrased a Bible passage, *"Get behind me, Satan,"* and threatened to bring down the plane until he was finally subdued by passengers. The man suffers from bi-polar disorder. Note that he didn't make any references to Darwin or Carl Sagan.

These unfortunates should not be condemned for their actions. They are to be pitied. Perhaps one day science, the proclaimed enemy by fundamentalist religionists, will find a cure for their ailments. One can only wonder if the fear of that cure is a reason for religionists' distrust and rejection of science. Who knows?

Beyond these sufferers is the larger body of fundamentalist/radical religionist extremists. No specific clinical condition is tied to their obsession with the supernatural. Rather, it is some combination of early indoctrination/cultural imperative, fear of death, under-education, economic deprivation, the desire for social acceptance by a larger group, the fear of being ostracized by the prevailing majority, a lack of self-worth, and a life of personal failure. We can exclude their fundamentalist shamans for the purpose of this discussion. They are in a separate category.

In person these fanatics are easy to spot. They preach in the street, carry signs that say "John 3:16," knock on your door, and spew their delusion all over your doorstep. In church, they flop on the floor and speak gibberish or feign unconsciousness as if overcome with religious ecstasy. But on the Internet they also have special characteristics that set them apart from the "normal" theists, by which I mean those believers for whom faith is a personal comfort, not a weapon, political party, or all-encompassing raison d'être.

The following are some hallmark behaviors of these willing whackos-for-Jesus that you may recognize from Internet interactions:

- Rambling and repetitive streams of thought; conglomerations of disconnected concepts (i.e., references to Einstein, Nostradamus, Occam, Hitler in one sentence)

- Insisting they are being victimized by the minority, a persecution complex
- Threats or implied threats of physical violence or God's wrath
- Repetitive obsessive reference to death, dying, and everlasting torture (ours, not theirs)
- The lack of composition and sentence structure; long posts in a single paragraph; frequent use of uppercase letters; multiple exclamation marks; the omission of the letter "o" when spelling "G-d"
- The invention/redefinition of words
- Misuse/misunderstanding of scientific terminologies; interspersing pseudo-science with apologetics; inappropriate insertion of scientific references
- Misrepresenting or denial of genuine statistics or proven trends
- Quote mining of famous freethinkers to imply an endorsement of belief
- Grasping at mysticism and prophetic foolishness to bolster their belief
- Quoting of biblical verse in lieu of independent thought; use of biblical verse as "proofs" of anything
- Demanding that you read such and such a book, link, or view a given video
- Harboring the delusion that anyone cares what they say or that they have the power to influence the thinking of secularists with their ranting

What largely motivates this erratic behavior is anyone's guess. Fear, chemical imbalance of the brain, intensive early indoctrination, an apostle complex...

any could be the driver. To people who cannot establish rewarding, meaningful, or long-lasting relationships with human beings, their relationship with their imaginary Friend is all they have. To people who fail at life, career, or success (however one defines it), clinging to a delusion gives a vestige of meaning to their existence.

The thought of their archaic belief system being rendered irrelevant by reason and science is the worst possible outcome to their already failed lives. Although they project bravado and confidence intended to mask it, their fear and desperation is almost palatable through their manic scribbling and prosaic shouting. It may even substitute as a sexual release, but I'm only speculating.

One can only wonder what they perceive to be their ultimate goal given that their method invariably yields the same non-result. Isn't doing the same thing over and over again and expecting a different result a definition of insanity?

63

Hump Internalizes the King of Kings

03 May 2010

I can no longer deny my Lord and Savior. I did this very day partake in His Goodness. I ask you all to join me in The King's Prayer:

Verily when I hungered He fedith me.

When I thirsted He gave me carbonated drink.

When I lacked for sodium His fries satiated me with the salt of the Earth.

He anointith me with His trans-fat free oil.

Yea, though I drove to the window without funds He taketh my Amex Card.

His forever smiling countenance shines down upon me from my TV screen.

Surely His calories, carbs and fat content shall follow me all the days of my life; for my ass grows large like a fatted calf.

Amen

Some reasoned doubters may rightfully ask, *"But, Hump, there are lots of icons of fast food that you could embrace and worship. Why pick The King over all others?"* Oh, they of little taste! The answers are obvious and all around them if only they could open their hearts, minds, mouths, and cholesterol-clogged arteries to the Truth.

First, anyone who has taken communion with The King, tasted of His body, the A-1 Steak Burger (a registered trademark of His Supreme Holiness), felt His beefy juiciness and His tangy sauce upon their tongue would surely know that this is food from a King...not a clown.

Second, He gives us Free Will to "Have it Yahweh," even to choose between sides of fries and sides of onion rings, both drenched in the divine fat of His being.

Third, much as only a beast of the field would feed from a trough, so only the misguided followers of a dead, white-suited, mustachioed, un-resurrected old redneck would eat from a bucket. They follow a false god and shall some day choke upon the wishbone of the Great Deceiver.

Fourth, Wendy is the Whore of Babylon, with her prepubescent freckles, unbridled hair, and promise of juiciness that can barely be sopped with multiple napkins. Shame! Woe be upon those who partake of her temptress' wares!

Finally, The King sacrificed His head and His face and replaced it with an oversized molded plastic model for us in order to cleanse the world of creepy painted clown faces.

Hear Me, O readers!! Only the fool says in his stomach, "The King is not Lard," for to deny Him condemns you to eating burgers with a "special sauce," the origin and content of which only the Clown (Satan's minion, who shares a remarkable resemblance to the fiend in Stephen King's *It*) knows.

You've been warned. Now, go forth; have lunch; and may the King bless you, and provide you with extra packets of Heinz, the blood of His body. Ask and ye shall receive.

64

The Ten Commandments As the Basis for US Law

09 May 2010

I'm up to here (picture the height of my hump) with Xtians attributing US law to the Ten Commandments. The fact is they have absolutely zero to do with our laws.

There were three versions of the commandments. One was verbally dictated by Moses. The second was when he spent forty days on Mt. Sinai chiseling them into two stone tablets, which he promptly smashed in a rage. The third was a replacement for the ones Moses broke. Each set was different. The first set didn't even discuss murder or stealing until it hit the thirteenth commandment (Exodus 20:2-17) and had a total of seventeen commandments. The second set (Deut. 5:6-21) had twenty-one commandments. In the third set (Exodus 34:11-27), God added even more self-serving edicts and outdid himself with twenty-seven commandments. They are now pretty much shaken, stirred, blended, redacted, edited, and reorganized into what we call the Ten Commandments. Of course, very few Xtians are aware of this.

Yet Xtian fanatics insist the Ten Commandments of lore are the basis for Western civilization's and US law and demand they be placed on public property, in government facilities, given special reverence and consideration in violation of the prohibition against endorsement of any religion by the secular state. They try to pass it off as "history," not religion, in an effort to circumvent the First Amendment's Establishment Clause. One may thus reasonably posit that the first issue of *Playboy* is history (and ever so much more instructive.) Should it then justify being given equal space in our government buildings?

The first four commandments are self-serving ego trips and religious demands by their fictional Sky Daddy that are not anywhere in our Constitution. In fact, it would be a violation of the First Amendment if they were.

There are no laws requiring anyone to honor their parents, nor prohibiting being envious of your neighbor's property, or his wife, or his "ass"—also not in the Constitution (Commandments V, X).

While there are archaic laws in some states about adultery, it is a throwback to theist think. They are not enforced (and certainly not punished by stoning to death, as prescribed in Talmudic law), and are also omitted from our Constitution (Commandment VII).

Lying is not illegal either, only committing perjury while under oath in a court of law is it punishable by our laws, or lying to obstruct justice, or if it is deemed to be libelous. Let's give this one half-credit (Commandment IX).

So this leaves the prohibition against killing (theists say "murder") and stealing (Commandments VI, VIII). But both of these prohibitions predate Christianity and the Hebrew Bible, having been codified by the early Egyptians, Hindus (India), Babylonians (The Code of Hammurabi), and Chinese.

Finally, US law is based on English common law, which pre-dates the arrival of Christianity to Britain by two hundred years, as Thomas Jefferson so eloquently pointed out (http://www.stephenjaygould.org/ctrl/jefferson_cooper.html).

So what's the score? Out of the Ten Commandments only two and a half (murder, stealing, and specific forms of bearing false witness) are part of our law. They would exist without the Hebrew Ten Commandments based on pre-Christian English common law and basic precepts that gave order to societies all over the planet well before the story of Exodus was written.

Not one in ten thousand Christians will know this, understand this, or embrace this. It's just too full of historical fact and documented evidence. The proofs can be researched and verified by anyone with average intellect, an iota of curiosity, and interest in the truth. Unfortunately, these are attributes that are alien to many theists.

65

Myth of the Angry Atheist

13 May 2010

"**D**awkins and Hitchens are angry atheists as are so many atheist bloggers. Their style is off-putting to atheists, agnostics and theists alike and is detrimental to the spread of freethought."

I've heard that kind of criticism frequently from other atheists and agnostics. Most often it comes from our humanist and secular humanist brethren. I refer to these freethinkers as the *"pass no judgment, kinder, gentler, live-and-let-live"* branch of the atheist family tree, and that's fine.

However, I cannot abide their holier-than-thou attitude that we atheists who are vocal and confrontational are simply angry, and that this supposed anger represents a threat to the spread of free thought among believers.

What they frequently perceive as anger would be better described as frustration and disgust with theist non-think, theist rejection of prima fascia evidence of scientific truths and reality, and their acceptance of the falsehood of supernaturalism. It's the same kind of frustration/disgust one might feel for people who still believe a woman's place is in the home—that she should be kept uneducated, barefoot, and pregnant. The same frustration/disgust one has watching shameless/unscrupulous/bombastic shamans extract money from impoverished believers in exchange for useless faith-healing prayers. The same disgust I have for the Obama "birther" fanatics.

That's not to say that there are no attitudes and actions that arouse anger in atheists, especially those of us who are anti-theists. But this anger is directed at those *attitudes* and *actions* of some theists—not their belief per se.

Example: I have anger for the purveyors of anti-gay hate who proclaim themselves loving Christians dong the bidding of their loving God, yet stand against extending full rights to gays. I have anger toward Christian politicians who send us to war in the name of their God. I'm angry at those theists who distort history and deny science and try to impose their lies into our schools, government, and lives. I am angered by fringe Christian parents who withhold medical help from a dying child because the Bible told them so. And I reserve the right to be angered by churches whose blind eye toward and/or cover-up of the immoral acts of their employees enable pedophilia. I would express that same anger toward anyone, believer or non-believer, who would actively promote hate, subjugation, and lies, or who allow their delusions or position of authority to undermine our freedoms and degrade our Constitution.

That there are thinking people—humanist, secularist, agnostic, or atheist—who *do not* feel anger for those horrendous actions is a mystery to me. That theists or some freethinkers are put off by justifiable expressions of my disgust (in absurd belief) or my anger (toward unjust action) simply cannot be of any concern to me. Anyone who proposes that by suppressing one's sense of indignation and wrapping it in some warm and fuzzy cloak of genteel complacency, one is more prone to get fanatical religionists to stop their harmful acts and throw off their attitude of hateful prejudices and delusions mandated by God is suffering from a kind of delusion of their own.

The "angry atheist" is a myth. When I, when any atheist, expresses anger at the actions and attitudes of some religionists, it's not because I am an atheist; it's because I am a freedom-loving, thinking human being enraged by the unjust acts that mindless devotion to ignorance promotes. Period. I am a person of reason with a low tolerance for injustice. That I happen to be an atheist doesn't justify the label "angry atheist." One could just as well label me an "angry Moderate," "angry Independent," "angry retiree," "angry veteran," "angry defender of justice," and "angry American."

As the bumper sticker says, "*Well-behaved women rarely make history*"; similarly, it wasn't well-behaved atheists who won us the right to profess our non-belief openly, to have atheist organizations, blogs, and books without fear of retribution. It wasn't complacent respecters of British injustice who won us our independence.

To those who decry the outspoken, confrontational nature of activist atheists and anti-theists who call it like they see it; or to those who bemoan the in-your-face/tell-it-like-it-is style of Madalyn Murray O'Hair, Dawkins, Hitchens, or Harris who have done so much to pave the way for the spread and rise of open free thought, I say: "If thine eye offends thee, pluck it out" and suck it up.

66

Make *Everyone Draw Muhammad Day* an Annual National Stand Against Tyranny

17 May 2010

After the Prophet Muhammad was depicted on Comedy Central's *South Park* back in April, a Muslim website threatened the producers with death. Oh, not in so many words ...they just posted a warning that what happened to Dutch filmmaker Theo Van Gogh might just befall them.

Van Gogh had the unmitigated nerve to depict Muhammad in one of his films. That blasphemy cost him his life at the hands of a follower of the "Religion of Peace." Kurt Westergaard, the Danish cartoonist who drew unflattering cartoons of Mohammed a few years back, is still under threat of a death *fatwa* and is in hiding. Just last week, Swedish artist Lars Vilks, who drew Muhammad as a dog in 2007, was assaulted during a lecture by a Muslim who was part of the group seeking to punish him. Vilks is a professor of art theory at the University of Uppsala in Sweden.

Comedy Central, showing all the courage of a rabbit, censored subsequent broadcasting of the Muhammad character storyline, effectively caving in to the threats of extremist Muslims. After all, no American has ever risked their life for free speech; why should Comedy Central be the trendsetters? Wait…lots of Americans have fought and died for our right to free speech! Oh, well, never mind.

In an admirable display of ballsiness, Seattle cartoonist Molly Norris asked fellow illustrators all over America to show their solidarity in support of free speech as granted under the First Amendment, to stand up to those troglodytes who would impose their will and truncate our rights with threat and innuendo. She suggested that on May 20, 2010, cartoonists draw and display their depictions of the Prophet Muhammad. Unfortunately, fearing for her life, Norris wimped out and backed off her suggestion.

I'm not a cartoonist, but I am an advocate for free speech, no matter whom it offends. In this country, free speech isn't just for speech you like or agree with, but this is lost on the followers of Muhammad. This is America, not seventh-century Saudi. I don't, none of us should, kowtow to the demands of those to whom free speech is but a phrase and who value ignorant superstition over one of our most cherished rights. Ben Franklin is credited with saying: *"They who can give up essential liberty to obtain a little temporary safety, deserve neither liberty nor safety."*

I'll give up not a speck of my liberty. I'll not be coerced into silence by religious fanatics. No amount of threat will force me to abandon my rights, nor will it succeed in imposing respect for their senseless religious precepts, prohibitions, and medieval culture. I will post pictures of Muhammad to my blog on May 20.

So, now what? *Fatwa? Jihad?* Am I to become camel hummus for Achmed and Abdul tonight? Here's a suggestion for the thug followers of the pedophile prophet and purveyor of ignorance, enslavement, and oppression:

"Pound sand...this is America!"

I hope this statement for freedom and against religious coercion becomes an annual national event. It's already on my calendar for next May.

67

Texas Makes Bid for Title of Most Religiously Oppressed State

24 May 2010

Permit me to first say to my Lone Star State freethinking readers that I can imagine living in one of the country's most religious regions is no picnic. Retaining your residence, not to mention your sanity, earns you my respect and sympathy. That said...

The Texas School Board voted to rewrite, distort, and otherwise degrade their social studies textbooks statewide. These Bible-banging, right-wing, bornagain Christians have decided that Thomas Jefferson was being given too much credit for his influence. The new version of their schoolbook downplays Jefferson's role and the entire concept of the separation of Church and State as guaranteed under the First Amendment, and which was subsequently confirmed by the Supreme Court. The book will proclaim that the US was a Christian nation founded on Christian values (I assume that means we as a nation endorse killing fig trees, conducting exorcisms, infecting herds of pigs with demons, and encouraging horse thievery—all New Testament values).

Their changes also give Ronald Regan and Newt Gingrich the kind of coverage previously reserved only for the greatness of Lincoln and our Founding Fathers. It implies that the McCarthy Communist witch hunt of the '50s was justified. It devotes pages of accolades to Confederate leaders and decries the United Nations as imperiling America's sovereignty.

What Texas high school students will now get is an education not from an impartial factual historical perspective, but from the fanatical perspective of far-right conservative fundamentalist religionists. Lucky them. As if Texas wasn't already a hotbed of religious delusion and blind devotion to stupidity...now their children will be receiving a religio-political rewrite of our nation's history.

Texas has historically set the standard for schoolbooks. Since they have such a large population of school kids, publishers typically use the same books for school districts all over the country. Already some states have moved to block the Texas version of US history so as not to infect their states with Texan insanity, ostensibly putting the publisher on notice that this version will not be accepted in their schools.

What's next? My guess is some Bible Belt states will enthusiastically endorse the Texas version of revisionist history. And now that the door has been cracked by a fanatical Christian majority school board, my guess is that Texas science books will eventually be perverted to include rebuttals to Big Bang and evolutionary theory: Creationism, Intel-Design, Young Earth-ism, Noah's flood carving out the Grand Canyon, resurrection of the old "missing link" bugaboo…who knows how far these mindless religious fanatics will go?

I've said it before, I'll say it again—they should change Texas' oft used insipid tag line from *"Don't mess with Texas"* to *"Don't mess with Texas—we're already as fucked up as we can get."*

68

End Priestly Celibacy? Let's Hope Not

28 May 2010

CNN reports that a dozen Italian women have written an open letter to the pope asking him to rescind the celibacy requirement for priests. They cite illicit relationships by priests as being rampant and call the ruling a man-made law (as though there are other kinds of laws other than the natural laws of science) [http://www.cnn.com/2010/WORLD/europe/05/28/italy.catholics.celibacy/index.html?hpt=T2].

All over the Internet the general consensus is that this would be a good thing. I couldn't disagree more.

The Catholic clergy celibacy rule has been a factor in the inability of the Catholic Church to attract new shaman recruits. They are already having problems getting enough priests to staff churches all over the US, resulting in churches being shut down and consolidated. Thus, celibacy works in our favor over the long run. Between priest shortages, a pedophile-enabling Catholic hierarchy, and their obscene position on discouraging condoms in third world AIDS-ravaged countries, the Catholic Church has never been closer to implosion. Relax the celibacy rule? Why fix what's not broken, or what is broken and should remain that way?

Some people say that allowing priests to have a normal sex life would eliminate or reduce pedophilia among the clergy. Nonsense! Pedophiles don't stop abusing children just because they are given permission to marry and boff consenting adults. Lots of pedophiles are married. Besides, do we really want these purveyors of medieval ignorance reproducing, mentally infecting their offspring, and repopulating the Church? I don't.

To counter these women's heretical suggestion, I plan to write a letter to the pope telling him I support celibacy for the priesthood. Further, that if the Church abandons its long-held and proper conviction and the celibacy requirement is relaxed, I will melt down my gold cross with the miniature Jesus on it, pound my Mary on a Half-Shell into plaster dust, auction off my collection of saintly memorabilia, and become a Methodist...or, worse, a JW.

Now, who's the pope going to listen to: a dozen horny women who are obviously after some priestly nookie, or a devout Catholic man who knows the evils of carnal lust? For the pope, I figure that would be a no-brainer (no pun intended).

69

"Dear Beloved in Jesus, Do I Have a Deal for You!"

07 Jun 2010

"*D*ear Beloved. Greetings in the name of God. May the blessings of God be upon you and grant you the wisdom to understand this situation and how much I need your help."

The above is the opening greeting from a typical email I receive two or three times a month to a couple of my email accounts. You may receive them as well, or perhaps my cruising of Xtian sites and blogs makes me especially attractive.

Invariably the letter purports to be from an old Christian widow woman who is dying from cancer and, for reasons known only to her and Jesus, she selected me to oversee the charitable distribution of her ten-million-dollar estate. In return, I will be rewarded with one-third of her holdings for my trouble. What a deal!

Although her residence varies, currently she claims residency in Saudi and, based on how long I've been getting these, she has been in the throes of death for some two or three years now.

The letter is long and crammed full of references to Jesus, heaven, finding her reward, blessings, and is signed, *"Yours in a Loving Christ"* or some such nonsense. It seems all that is required is my full name, address, and phone number to get things going. Occasionally I reply to these emails, wishing the poor woman a lingering and hideous death, and promising her that Satan and I will be happy to double-team her when she reaches her reward in hell...I being the one with the hump and the enormous member. Much to my disappointment, I never get a reply.

What's fascinating about this is the assumption that by invoking Jesus and tossing out endless Christian platitudes, the target will be swayed to participate in this blatantly transparent scam. I'm guessing they meet with some success with this strategy since the letters haven't changed very much in two years.

Why Christians? The scammers obviously see Christians as particularly open to being ripped off by anyone sharing their beliefs. They are well aware that Christians have abandoned all common sense, opting to believe the most ridiculous things on faith. Plus, they are scammed every Sunday when they drop their money into the old collection plate at church. Since America is a hot bed of fundamentalist delusion, they also assume that every one of the thousands upon thousands of Americans they email is a believer ripe for the picking.

What is my evidence for my hypothesis? Not once have I received an email offer from a wealthy dying woman addressed to *"Dear Reasoned and Rational Free-thinker."* Go figure.

70

"God Loves You, and God Is Good": Oh, Really?

17 Jun 2010

"*God loves you, and God is good*" was the reassuring comment from a religionist on a Facebook discussion thread. She was defending her imaginary sky friend from a withering attack by a couple of atheists discussing the uselessness of religion.

My reply to that bland and predictable Christian throwaway line was: *"Good for what, precisely?"* No answer was tendered by this self-appointed publicist for her God.

I suppose if one never read the Old Testament, avoided biblical criticism, and simply fast-forwarded through the New Testament without giving their God's behavior much thought, one could pick out a few dozen verses that were good, maybe even loving, if not unique to Christianity.

But as we all know, the god described in that hideous tome exposes itself to be overwhelmingly a vengeful, murdering, genocidal, sexually obsessed, misogynistic, homophobic, brutal, slavery-endorsing, self-centered, arbitrary, cruel, contradictory, and confused tyrannical psychopath.

Had that Christian PR woman bellied up to the bar and not just pulled the pin, tossed a platitude, and run, I'd have challenged her to a duel of verses. For every verse she provided that implies a good and loving God, I would match her with one and a half verses that demonstrate it to be an evil and hateful deity. All she would be left with is trying to defend her position with desperately weak platitudes such as:

- *"But they had it coming—they were an evil* [pick one or more] *culture, religion, civilization; a mean group of children; uppity women; horrid witches; unclean animals; expendable offspring."* She would be in the position of having to defend the inexcusable by rationalization that she could never employ in a secular, modernistic world.
- *"You're taking it out of context."* However, she won't be able to offer the context that makes it good and justifiable by any ethical standard.
- *"God works in strange and mysterious ways/who are we to know or understand God's plan?"* Last-resort cop-out. If her God's intent and actions confuse her, and more is implied than its actions at face, how can she profess to know God has a plan, that its planned intent is good, or that it loves anything other than itself? That leaves her only *"the Bible tells me so"*...circular thinking / argument and admission of defeat.

Maybe she saw this coming, had experienced it before, and opted out of the challenge, hoping her one-liner hit and run would, by the grace of God, win some converts.

I for one wouldn't want to be loved by this hideous beast of a god. After all, it manifests its love in rather unhealthy ways. It loved all its original creations, all their offspring, all those animals, everyone who doesn't believe in it, its very own son...and look what it did or threatens to do to them. Nah, if such an evil being were real and we couldn't kill it, I'd rather it just ignored me or didn't know I existed.

71

Hump's Dog Explains Her Trip to the Other Side

21 Jun 2010

My Staffordshire terrier, Ella, is fourteen years old. On medication for congestive heart failure, she also has various other infirmities, discomforts, and peculiarities associated with being ninety-eight years old in dog years. These include but are not limited to a congenital bladder infection, thus occasional incontinence, a lack of discrimination as to where she defecates, and a tendency to inexplicably bark at trees, chairs, and nothing in particular.

From time to time she also tends to arbitrarily feign death, or at least to pull the old Redd Foxx *"I'm coming, Elizabeth"* dramatic dying routine, sending Mrs. Hump and I into a tizzy. This morning Ella bought the farm…again, or so she says.

I called the vet when Ella's legs collapsed from under her. She was panting rapidly and her tongue started to turn blue. We agreed he'd come and help her die comfortably at home as soon as his office hours finished at noon.

Ella lay quietly on the big pillow on our covered porch while my wife stroked her head and I rubbed her belly, dripping water into her mouth from a rubber syringe. Ella's eyes were closed; her breath became more shallow and even. It didn't look like she'd make it until noon. We solemnly waited for death to come.

Forty-five minutes later, she was eating a bowl of chopped meat, lapping up water, and taking in the smells, sights, and sounds of rural New Hampshire from her porch perch. Ambling down the steps, she casually emptied her bowels on my perfectly manicured lawn. She was back to normal.

"WTF, Ella!!?" I demanded. "I figured you for dead!"

"You sound disappointed," she passively retorted.

"No, of course not—but you came THIS close to your final vet's visit," I said, holding my fingers a Milk Bone's width apart.

"You know I hate that son-of-a-bitch; he always smells like he's had his arm up a cow's ass. And what happened to our 'do not resuscitate' agreement?"

"Uh, yeah...but he wasn't coming to resuscitate you."

She was nonplused by this. She's been around long enough to know that I wouldn't rush her demise any more than I would delay it if her quality of life took a major, irreversible, downward turn.

Ella yawned and let out a series of barks for no reason in particular. "You needn't have bothered. I was ostensibly dead," she casually offered.

"No, you weren't. You were just, I dunno, having one of your old dog moments. And if you died, how is it you're not dead now?" I challenged.

She pondered this for a moment, head cocked to the side.

"It wasn't my time, I guess. But the experience was as vivid as that dump on the lawn. My whole life rushed before my eyes, from puppyhood right 'til this morning. Next thing I know I was in a big, open, sun-lit field. Hey, remember the cocker spaniel you had before me? Well, she was there. She asked how you were doing. I told her about your weight gain. And there were lots of other dogs running around sniff-ing each other's butts, chasing balls, chewing on steak bones. Then some nice old guy came out with chopped meat and fresh water and we all chowed down while the cool morning breeze blew across our ears and some babe stroked my head." She closed her eyes and smiled a satisfied dog smile.

"Wait a damn second!" I protested. *"What are you saying—that there's an afterlife, a doggie heaven? That my rejection of ancient myth and the supernatural is wrong? That my acceptance of natural law and reality was a mistake? That everything I have come to accept as reasoned and logi-cal is now completely null and void?"* Ella could tell I was becoming agitated.

"Hey, Big Guy...don't get your flea collar in a knot! Did you hear me say anything about heaven or an afterlife? You're a semi-educated human; haven't you heard about the effect of oxygen deprivation, endor-phins, various other brain chemicals and how they cause vivid memories and hallucinations in near-death situations?"

I was embarrassed. Of course I understood these things. They have been studied and understood by the medical profession for years. I chalked up my emotional overreaction to the stressful events of the morning.

"Besides," she added, "after fourteen years I thought you knew me better. What do you take me for, a brain-damaged cat, or worse, a damn theist?"

72

For God So Loved the World That He Gave His Creations Flesh-Eating Bacteria and Ebola

01 Jul 2010

Christians love to invoke "free will" for all kinds of things. They say homosexuality is a choice. That God gives free will, and gays chose to be gay just like the rest of us chose heterosexuality (you remember when you chose to be hetero, right?). They have to say that. If they accept a genetic predisposition toward homosexuality it would mean that their God endorsed homosexuality, that homosexuality is just as natural as can be. There can be none of that. After all, the Bible says homosexuality is an abomination and God doesn't create abominations. Q.E.D., homosexuality has to be man's poor use of his God-given free will. End of discussion.

But what happens when Christians come face to face with conditions where free will and man's choice cannot be easily invoked to explain away "abominations"? Why do people come down with ALS, aka

Lou Gehrig's disease, arguably the most hideous fatal genetic disease one could possibly imagine? No one chooses ALS. Nothing one does from a behavioral, ethical, or moral perspective is known to cause ALS. So if God created man in his image, and God doesn't screw things up, what does this all mean—that God has ALS and wanted us to have it too? Or that their God creates hideous diseases to torment and torture his creations as he tortured himself through his son? And why—out of love? What sane being knowingly gives someone a torturous fatal disease out of love, or for any reason?

Why did their God, who created all life, create Necrotizing fasciitis, aka flesh-eating bacteria? Why did their God create the virus that causes Ebola hemorrhagic fever? These life forms cause horrible suffering and death to thousands of people every year—no free will choice involved. Is it punishment for being a third-world infant? Is it retribution for some African toddler's childish insult to a prophet or to God itself? Does God punish children to death for the free will choices of their parents? What kind of sane being punishes the innocent child for the adult's trespasses?

This problem, which cannot be explained away by free will, provokes all kinds of mental gymnastics among the pious. I once had one of them tell me that such God-given diseases "build character." I wanted very badly to help build that cretin's character with a pipe-wrench-induced blood clot to his head.

"Suffering of the innocent is part of a bigger plan that we cannot understand" is among the most favored platitudes/non-explanations/pious   cop-outs/denials of logic and irrational retorts. It requires of them no analysis of the issue. It does not make them face the challenge of the paradox head on. It is escape into mindless babble to avoid what common sense screams at them from just below the surface of their enslaved minds. It does exactly what it has to do when self-imposed ignorance comes face to face with reason...it ends discussion.

73

The Holy Prophylactic:
Let Jesus Be Their Condom

06 Jul 2010

I've been having a pen pal exchange with my Christian author friend in Canada. Some of his comments caused me to wince. While he is an educated fellow, his ability to see things outside of "religious think" in a broader perspective with full rationality is tenuous, at best.

We've been discussing the Catholic Church's doctrine against condoms. I suggested that he should take a stand against that policy, which has been complicit in the deaths of millions in third-world countries, especially Africa. (My words are in italics.)

"FOR ME TO EXPECT PEOPLE WHO BELIEVE IN ABSTINENCE TO GO PASSING OUT CONDOMS IS LIKE ME EXPECTING YOU TO PASS OUT BROCHURES ON 'THE FOUR SPIRITUAL LAWS.'"

Maybe that's the difference between Christians and secularists. If handing out The Four Spiritual Laws was scientifically correlated to the prevention of suffering and death for

*millions of men women and children due to AIDS, it would
be unethical for me not to support it and morally deficient by
not working to get others to do the same.*

*To remain silent, to throw up one's hands, to not speak out
against an irrational prohibition based on the non-scriptural
interpretation of ancient superstitious doctrine is tantamount
to tacit approval of the Catholic Church's death-dealing policy.*

"I'M NOT EVEN A CATHOLIC. I'VE BEEN
USING CONDOMS UNTIL I STARTED SHOOT-
ING BLANKS SO THIS IS A LITTLE NUTTY TO
ME. HOW MANY CONDOMS ARE YOU HANDING
OUT?"

*This isn't about you or me. It's about millions of third-
world people to whom the words of the Catholic Church are
sacrosanct and they are dying because of it. The Catholic
Church's position is as nutty and as unholy as it can be. That
you seem so cavalier about it is disappointing.*

Finally this:

"CONDOMS ARE [ONLY] 90% EFFECTIVE...
THERE'S A 10% CHANCE YOU'LL DIE, GO FOR IT.
OFFERING CONDOMS MAY HELP SOME...BUT...
WHAT I'VE SEEN IS TRUE CHANGE HAPPENS
WHEN ONE GENUINELY FOLLOWS THE FOOT-
STEPS OF JESUS. IN OTHER WORDS, THE SCREW-
ING AROUND STOPS, DADS COME HOME, THE
WOMEN ARE CARED FOR, ETC."

*If you agree that condoms are 90% effective, your lack
of condemnation of this Catholic prohibition is even more
disconcerting. If we can't have 100% proven protection, we
shouldn't work toward 90%? If 90% is better than 0%,
should we deny it to them and rely solely on Christian teach-
ings/abstinence/Jesus to restrain the natural human sex drive?
That's as obscene a lack of reason and rejection of reality as I
could imagine.*

The thousands of sexually promiscuous and child-molesting pastors and priests, the so-called Christian Values politicians caught time and time again with their morals hanging out, the high rate of teen pregnancies in our most religious states all are witness to the power of the human sex drive and Jesus' impotence as a prophylactic.

Along with the highest teen pregnancy rate, the USA has the highest divorce rate in the West. Yet we have the most religious population in the industrialized world. Sarah Palin's born-again daughter's pregnancy was a result of her mother's abstinence-only non-think indoctrination and denial of the natural sex urge. What when wrong? They should have had "more faith"? Do we chalk it up to Satan?

Until this irrational doctrine of abstinence only/"just come to Jesus" is thrown into the trash heap of mindless, simplistic, and failed teachings, Christianity in general and Catholicism in particular are complicit in the spread of this disease among those least equipped to fight it.

I don't expect to get my author pal to come around to logic untainted by Christian delusion. It seems even some Christians to whom condom use is a legitimate birth control and disease preventative devise for their use won't condemn the Catholic Church's mindless prohibition. Even they opt for Jesus as the preferred prophylactic for third-world, impoverished peoples. Evidently what works for the white North American Christian isn't effective for black African Christians. I don't like what that implies.

Too much Jesus on one's mind is a horrible thing.

74

The Comfort of God's Orderly Creation:
The Horror of a Random Universe

11 Jul 2010

IN THE BEGINING Man's understanding of science, his comprehension of the universe and the forces of the physical world were miniscule. Just as we ask ourselves "why and how," so did the ancients ponder the mysteries of what they observed.

Today we answer those questions with the benefit of thousands of years of accumulated knowledge augmented by the past three hundred years' explosive scientific discoveries. The ancients answered the questions the best they could within the context of their culture and personal experience. All knowledge and experience was predicated on one thing: the universe was there for Man's benefit. Everything in their realm of consciousness was species-centric.

Since every primitive technology they had was a creation of Man, surely everything they did not/could not create had to be formed by a more powerful Creator. And if the social construct included rule by a king, then surely there was a higher unseen king/god or gods who demanded fealty and obedience in exchange for his gifts and omnificence. It was only "logical."

Every earthquake, flood, lightning strike, eclipse was a sign or omen. Every successful hunt and every failed hunt, every bountiful harvest and every failed crop, every victory in battle and every defeat was due to a god's hand—a sign of its presence and affirmation of its relationship with Man, a sign of his pleasure or displeasure.

Everything in the sky was meant to serve Man, for why else would it exist? The moon differentiated periods of time, segmenting the seasons in a predictable pattern...all for Man's benefit. The stars and the moon gave light to better see at night...all for Man's benefit. The Sun was a life force, possibly a god unto itself...all for Man's benefit. These things could only be designed for and presented to Man by a beneficent Being who interacts with his creations—rewarding them when he/she/it was happy and proud of them, and meting out punishment when they broke the societal taboos, which offended it.

When in doubt as to a god's actions, the shaman was consulted. He knew the gods' reasoning. He'd interpret it and give guidance. Invariably penance in the form of a burnt offering of grain, animal, or human flesh would set things right. It was orderly. All the mysteries of the observable universe were understood; nothing had to be unknown—if Man didn't do it, the god or gods did. It made perfect sense. What could be more comforting?

And what could be more horrifying than the obverse possibility—that all is not guided by Super Being(s) just for Man's benefit or a Super Being's own satisfaction? What if there was no guiding force with whom they could reason, to whom they could implore, in whom they could trust to control their lives and world? How would they have rationalized an infinitely expanding universe that extends beyond their view, even beyond their imagination, all without any impact on Man and his world? How could the chaos and randomness of asteroid, meteor, and comet impacts on billions of worlds billions of light years away be reconciled with the orderliness of a universe devised just for Man? Why would billions of suns shine their light and life-sustaining heat on worlds that Man does not inhabit? How could the Earth, Sun, water, atmosphere, all plant and animal life not have been specially supplied to Man by the hand of that Being, and instead be the result of a massive explosion of chaos, random combination of natural forces and elements, and the evolutionary process?

To the Creationist religionists of today, just as it was with the ancients, the orderly guiding hand of a Super God King who made all, sees all, controls all, and must be obeyed is still the great comfort. The chaos, randomness, and uncontrolled actions by mindless physical forces of the natural universe are the antithesis of orderliness and comfort, a horror that must be shunned and denied.

In spite of all we have learned, which has whittled away to but a splinter what our Bronze Age predecessors fully attributed to their Super Being God King, the remnants of that belief continue to control some twenty-first-century minds.

That's the real horror.

75

Those Damnable "New Atheists"

21 Jul 2010

The Reverend Paul Prather is a Kentucky minister, sometime blogger, and contributor to his local newspaper. He is also a whiner and has a stunted ability to think much beyond his limited worldview and his caricature of non-religionists.

Recently he wrote an article entitled *"New atheists embody the very things they hate."* It's his rant against "new atheism," a term that religionists wield against twenty-first-century atheists like an epithet, much as Muslim *jihadists* use "infidel" for all non-Muslim Westerners, or like Christians use "Christ killer" for Jews.

The following are a few extracts from his misguided essay[*], which will serve as examples of theists' shortsightedness and myopic perspective of what atheism is all about.

---

[*]   Rev. Prather's article in full: http://www.kentucky.com/2010/06/12/1303777/paul-prather-new-atheists-embody.html#ixzzotkmOZZ10

"My objection to the new atheists isn't that they're atheists. It's that they strike me as hypocrites, which is the charge they unfailingly level, with mixed justification, against the religious. In opposing religion in the manner they do, they betray themselves as possessing the traits they profess to loathe."

Hypocrites? Perhaps he thinks we *do* believe in a god or gods when we say we do not? Maybe we say we oppose intolerance of homosexual rights but really go out and try to make gays' lives miserable? Perhaps we really *do* reject the proofs of science deep down and are just professing it to appear erudite? We don't even go door to door trying to deprogram theists. Hypocrites? I don't get it.

As I have said often, I don't oppose religion per se. I oppose the *product* of theistic thought, that which impedes scientific progress, limits personal freedoms, uses belief to justify political extremism, including theocracy, terror, and war. I'll oppose anything that seeks to enslave minds to ancient views of reality and morality that are defunct. Any religionists who do not subscribe to those things are not targets of my "opposition." The reverend continues...

"...they cherry-pick historical examples of religious wrongdoing while ignoring the innumerable instances in which the faithful have performed great acts of decency and charity."

When acts of theistic decency have to be trotted out as a counterpoint to the acts of religiously instigated wrongdoing, it begs a cost-benefit analysis. I'd proffer that if the evils wrought by religion are laid on the scale of judgment alongside the contributions of religion to the advancement of civilization and human existence, the evils would heavily tilt the scale.

What benefits have been derived from religionists because of their superstition that could counteract centuries of God-inspired genocide by the Hebrew tribes, or two thousand years of Church-inspired persecution of the Jews or worldwide Muslim terrorist bombings, or the misrepresentation of the value of condoms, or all the deaths attributable to intra-sect warfare through the ages? Do the good intentions of Mother Theresa or the Salvation Army negate them? How about the acts of the Legion of Christ or Opus Dei? "Cherry-pick" means to select that which satisfies an agenda, while intentionally leaving the rest behind. Religionist examples of wrongdoing defy cherry-picking the evidence, for it will be in today's newspaper.

"I wish these atheists would venture...into a seminary library. They'd find tens of thousands of volumes written by thinkers great and obscure across two millennia."

No doubt true. But careful examination of the contributions of theists in real-world terms (i.e., science and medicine by notable theists like Gregor Mendel, Christian Barnard, Jonas Salk, Albertus Magnus, Robert Grosseteste, Roger Bacon, and other personages of faith) shows that they were made *in spite* of their theism, not *because* of it. Had they not extended themselves beyond the precepts of their religious indoctrination and the ignorant falsehoods of scripture, they'd have contributed much less.

Look, this "new atheist" label that seems to have aroused the ire of the theist majority is simply a cover for religionists' disgust with or fear of the fact that activist atheists have decided not to hide in the closet any longer. We no longer are content to be anonymous observers standing idly by while religion drags civilization back into the Dark Ages or destroys lives and minds. "New atheist" is theist code for *"...those uppity, mouthy atheists who aren't content to hide from the Inquisi-*

tion like in the good old days, refuse to kowtow to the Chris-
tian majority, and who insist on using reason and science
openly to make us look like the backward superstionalists that
we are."

For once, they're absolutely right.

76

The Beauty and Nobility of Misery and Suffering: A Disturbing Revelation

26 Jul 2010

In a follow-up to our ongoing exchange of emails, my Canadian Christian author friend asked me this about my feelings on AIDS deaths in Africa:

"I'm very intrigued to know if you've considered why all of this matters so much to you."

I found this shocking. Before replying, I gave this a great deal of thought, which brought me to a horrifying revelation. Here is my response.

Dear P,

You wonder why the issue of millions dying of AIDS in Africa is of such importance to me. To me and to all realists, the life we have is the only one we'll ever have. Thus we value it highly. Unlike Mother Teresa, who said, "The suffering of the poor is something very beautiful and the world is being very much helped by the nobility of this example of misery and suffering," *a mindset which I find obscene and perverse, we the thinking see no beauty, no nobility, no glory in the suffering and death of innocent people. That's why the issue is so important to me.*

But your question caused me to have a revelation of sorts. These poor, uneducated, third-world people are falsely told by the pope that condoms do more harm than good and that the path to ending this epidemic is "belief" and devoting oneself to the ghost of some presumed ancient mystic-cum-Man-god. But the Catholic Church and any Christian who downplays the importance of condom use, favoring instead acceptance of Jesus, doesn't much care about the suffering or death of the millions. The words of Mother Teresa are proof of that.

What they, what you, care about, what your agenda is, what all your efforts are directed toward is converting people to Jesus..."saving souls." If for every one million people who die because of lack of sex education and unavailability of condoms, a dozen souls can be brought to Jesus, then it's a small price to pay. Human life and the avoidance of suffering isn't precious to people like you, the pope, or Mother Teresa because to your kind this life is but a staging ground, preparation, a test of sorts for the "real reward" in your fictional heaven.

Oh, yes, you and they pay it lip service. You'll praise the missionaries for mopping the sweating brow of a dying AIDS child. You'll wring your hands and shed crocodile tears over the multitude that will die today. You'll protest that Christians have done so much to ease their suffering in the throes of death. But the reality is these lives are being sacrificed on the altar of religious ignorance...for a "higher purpose." Their lives aren't precious—their souls and the afterlife take precedence.

P, in my last email I called you cavalier about the millions dying of AIDS. I was wrong. Cavalier doesn't begin to describe it. You and those who think this way are knowingly complicit in their deaths.

You want to save their souls? Then save their only life with proven science first THEN do your evangelical proselyt-

izing thing. To do otherwise is akin to a doctor withholding proven treatment, substituting it with a lecture about watching his cholesterol and getting more exercise while the man is dying from a massive heart attack. It's immoral.

Now I don't mean to offend, and I value our friendship; but I think I am on to something here that I expect you will protest and dismiss as totally fallacious. I'll understand that. Nevertheless, I've come to know the Christian mind pretty well through my many readings and over many years of discourse. I dare say that it would be impossible for you or others who think in these terms to openly admit as true what I have come to realize (at long last) is clearly at the very root of this whole issue.

It disturbs me. I wish it disturbed you.

77

A Camel's Prayer: Please Join Me in Worship

01 Aug 2010

Please prostrate yourself and join me in prayer to some supernatural being of your imagination.

O, **Supernatural Higher Intellect of The Highly Unlikely Existence**—thou art the be all and end all, the Alpha and the Omega, the zenith and the dregs, the apex and the slit trench. I am but a lowly life form of your creation, although a lot better than a tapeworm. I worship you because I know you love me and also because I know if I don't worship you that you have the power to subject me to eternal torture forever, withholding the release of death, or even to turn me into a tapeworm, for thou art Omnipotent.

[Congregation in unison] *"Praise be to You, O Lord. Please don't hurt me and thank you for not making me an intestinal parasite."*

O, **Supernatural Higher Intellect of The Highly Unlikely Existence (aka, SHITHUE)**—I am humbled before your greatness, for I am nothing. Everything I eat I owe to you, and not to me, the farmers, or the

Wal-Mart Super Store double-coupon promotion. Everything I own was your doing, and not mine. My career, my promotion, my 401K, my retirement, my wife and children, my health insurance, my new fifty-two-inch flat screen TV …all is through your largess and generosity. Without you I would regress into a primitive subhuman groveling in the muck, raping, killing, stealing, molesting, and voting for godless Democrats (aka, Communists; aka, the Anti-You).

[Congregation in union] *"Praise be to You, O Lord. Thank you for holding my health insurance co-pay to twenty-five dollars per visit. "*

O, S H I T H U E—please hear my prayer. Smite mine enemies. Strike them down. Blind them. Make them suffer. Infect their pets with fleas and their children with head lice. You know who they are, for thou art Omniscient. Your creation of Tay Sachs Syndrome and Sickle Cell Anemia are a good start and doth comfort me.

[Congregation in unison] *"Praise be to You, O Lord, healer of head colds, bringer of rain…eventual stopper of oil spills, protector and deliverer of Your righteous followers, and uncompromising plague-inducing/death-dealing ogre to all others and sometimes Your own blood relatives."*

O, S H I T H U E—Thou art pure goodness and love, and yet I inexplicably fear Your unpredictable sociopathic wrath and Cower in your Gory for ever and ever.

[Congregation in unison] *"Praise be to You, O Lord, Omni-benevolent and loving destroyer, and hater of amputees."*

Amen

[Congregation in unison] *"Amen."*

The faithful who would like to partake in Holy Communion and receive the host, please form a line down the center aisle. And please, people...those of you with oral herpes, don't let your open sores ooze into the punch bowl of the Lord's blood, and no double-dipping into the mango salsa of the Lord's body. Thank you.

78

Those Damn Homos Are Changing Word Definitions! Stop Them NOW!

10 Aug 2010

Tony Perkins is the head of the Family Research Council. The organization is, to put it bluntly, ultra-conservative, ultra-Christian, and ultra-homophobic. He and they would love nothing more than to see America ruled by cross-wielding religious fanatics who'd replace the Constitution with the Bible, making the Inquisition look like the Campfire Girls' summer camp.

Recently Tony raged against the overturning of Prop 8 in California. He made these two statements:

"The fact that homosexuals prefer not to enter into marriages as historically defined does not give them a right to change the definition of what a 'marriage' is"; "FRC has always fought to protect marriage in America and will continue to do so by working with our allies to appeal this dangerous decision" (http://www.frc.org/newsroom/frc-criticizes-court-rul-ing-warns-against-the-roe-v-wade-of-same-sex-marriage).

Protect marriage? Protect it from what, exactly? My marriage doesn't require his protection; whose does? I understand protecting children from clergy pedophiles, but how does one protect a word or concept from evolving and why? Besides, if Tony is protecting marriage, he's done a piss poor job of it considering the nation's 50% divorce rate.

Like all religious extremists, Tony is confused and living in denial. The "historic definition" of many words in the English lexicon is not static. Language evolves. I suppose he's still wringing his hands over the evolved "historic definition" of the word "gay." He and his ilk must have accepted it since I don't hear any of them saying things such as, *"I'm feeling particularly gay today."* I imagine they stay up nights bemoaning the evolution of the word "awful," which once meant "deserving of awe."

Sorry, Tony, but just like language, cultural mores evolve. Women can now own property—historically and biblically they couldn't. People can't own slaves—historically and biblically they could. Inter-racial couples, once deemed to be in violation of God's plan, can now marry—historically in the "Christian" US they couldn't. Being gay, committing adultery, and working on the "Sabbath" is no longer punishable by death—historically and biblically it was. You'll get used to gay marriage, Tony, just like you've gotten used to, or at least grudgingly accepted, these other examples of cultural evolution.

I keep asking why religionists insist on forcing selected/cherry-picked ancient Hebraic admonishments on society. How does the evolution away from these things directly negatively affect their lives, their freedoms? Why don't they rage against people wearing mixed fiber clothes (Lev. 19:19), or boiling a kid goat in its mother's milk (Exodus 23:14-19), and demand constitutional amendments to enforce them? In the absence of a satisfactory response, the only answer I can come up with is hypocrisy and hate born of the religious virus.

But it doesn't matter. In five to ten years, gay marriage will be legal in a majority of states. And in three hundred to five hundred years, the Christian churches will apologize for their homophobic hysteria. It just takes them that long to catch up to humanity.

79

Christians against the Jedi Religion and Smurfs: Maybe They Fear the Competition

15 Aug 2010

Recently the surge in people claiming to be adherents of the Jedi Religion (the *Star Wars* spiritual invention) was publicized in the media. The following is a verbatim comment made by a Christian in response to this phenomenon.

"Jedi Knights? We have traded reality for fantasy, the Kingdom of God for Disneyworld, smurfs for angels. I think I will stick with Jesus, the Son of the Living God, the undisputed, historically based Way, Truth, and Life, whose resurrection was witnessed by hundreds, whose martyrs number in the thousands, and followers in the millions over 2000 years. Any of these deceived Jedi warriors willing to lay down their lives for their 'leader.' Or do they have one? No wonder the world is such a mess with people's pop (poop) culture 'religions.' Give me Truth any day. The consequences are more predictable."

—Mark H.

Quite a rant. Naturally, I couldn't let Mark's comment go unchallenged. The only question was where to start:

Mark,

To paraphrase Yoda: *"Many statements of fallaciousness it is that you make."* Not one is supportable with objective evidence. By substituting "Allah" for God, "Paradise" for Kingdom, and "Allah's last prophet, Mohammed" for Jesus, ostensibly everything you wrote could be expressed by a Muslim.

Your acceptance of Christianity is as much based on fantasy as any other religion, past or present. Your acceptance and deification of Jesus is as valid as any other mythical man-god, supernatural force, or fabled creature, past or present. That it happens to be YOUR fantasy, YOUR creature is why you cannot discern the difference.

Jesus is *"undisputed"*? He's disputed by Hindus, Muslims, Jews, wiccans, animists, and every other religion on the planet, plus non-believers, which combined represent two-thirds of the Earth's population. It's only "undisputed" by you and your fellow Xtians.

The resurrection was witnessed by hundreds? Not according to the Bible, and the Bible would have mentioned eyewitnesses, had there been any. If you were alluding to the alleged observations of a post-death Jesus, it is undocumented anywhere except by the writers of the Bible, none of whom themselves were eyewitnesses to the so called resurrection or a post death appearance. They were simply passing on hearsay. This includes Paul, the recruiter and deluded public relations man for the cult—hardly an objective reporter. There are no other independent source documents that attest to seeing the resurrection itself or even a reanimated post-death Jesus out of the "hundreds" of witnesses you claim.

Dying for a myth and a lie is rather common. That the Holocaust claimed six million Jews doesn't attest to their faith being "true." That fifty-eight thousand Americans died in Vietnam didn't legitimize the "Domino Theory" of the spread of Communism. History has proven it to be an erroroneous concept, as we all see. That cultists drink cyanide-tainted Kool Aid or otherwise kill themselves for their belief or at the behest of their leaders doesn't validate their belief as being "true." If martyrdom were evidence of truth, then Muslims have as much claim to truth as do Christians. How telling that you'd be more generous and give the Jedi religion more respect and credence if some number of its followers would just die for their belief. This fascination and obsession with dying as a validation of belief is peculiar to the Abrahamic religions among all modern day religions. It has been the cause of much havoc through the ages.

As for "giving [you] the Truth," it's evident from your attributing the world's problems to a lack of shared belief in your preferred religious delusion that you neither want to hear nor can handle the truth. Your Christian "Truth" ruled the civilized world during the Dark and Middle Ages, and my guess is you'd not have wanted to live during those times—especially if you were a Jew, a non-believer, a non-warrior, or a serf.

Read more history; think more independently; broaden you understanding of religiosity beyond your own chosen cult; question what you're taught; live life on your feet and not on your knees. Your contributions to society would be the better for it. May the Farce of Religion not be with you.

80

CS Lewis: Deluded, Deceiver, or Dolt?

21 Aug 2010

CS Lewis was an author and a Christian defender of the faith in the early twentieth century. Famous for his *Chronicles of Narnia,* among other works, he was well educated and scholarly—the classic Christian apologist.

I say "classic" because his arguments for a "Real Morality" (i.e., God-given morality) and his famous *"Trilemma"* (we know it as his *"Jesus was either Liar, Lunatic, or Lord"* argument) are so vapid, so fallacious, so easily refutable though research, reason, and observation that only a Christian could perceive them as intellectual or worthy of repeating. One doesn't have to wonder too hard why Lewis's "Trilemma" wasn't a "Qinlemma," to include the possibility Jesus was *"Nonexistent, or a composite of various pre-Christian pagan gods".*

Although raised in a religious family, Lewis claimed he became atheist at the age of fifteen only to find Christianity again in his later years. But here's the thing: he claimed that as an atheist he was *"very angry with God for not existing."* Now, think about that. Can you conceive of yourself or anyone who rejects the concept of a god, attributing it to a man-made fallacy, being *"angry with God for not existing?"* It is antithetical to what atheism means, oxymoronic at best, patently absurd at worst. Atheist at fifteen? Fact is he and his father had a falling out and his claiming to be an athe-ist was his way of rebelling. It was a ploy.

Nevertheless, Christians love to name-drop Lewis, quote him, pull examples from his writings, and implore us to read his works. They use him as some kind of proof of Christianity's veracity. After all, an "atheist" becoming a Christian make him a rare commodity, a darling of the religiously enam-ored. It's a validation of their belief. I would venture that the insipid and hackneyed platitude *"You're just angry at God"* that Christians love to throw at atheists is attributable to CS Lewis' self-described anger with God as an "atheist." Now, there's a contribution to Christian apologetics.

Here's an example of a Lewis quote that would make any thinking person wince:

"If you read history you will find that the Christians who did most for the present world were precisely those who thought most of the next. It is since Christians have largely ceased to think of the other world that they have become so ineffective in this."

Two things are obvious to anyone with a modicum of intellectual awareness:

1) It is unsupportable opinion to state that strong belief in the afterlife has motivated the best contribu-tions to this civilization.

2) The premise is not intended to be challenged, researched, and evaluated for veracity because the examples that disprove it/falsify it are vast.

But that doesn't matter to believers. They take that kind of statement at face value...as a "Truth." They don't think for a moment, *What degree of belief in the afterlife did Copernicus have? Did Dr. Christiaan Barnard or Charles Darwin have?* They were Christians all, but not one sliver of historical and corroborated evidence exists that establishes their *degree* of belief in an afterlife. Indeed, there are many examples of Christians who whole-heartedly embraced belief in the afterlife whose hideous words, deeds, and legacies are renowned. Martin Luther comes to mind. His contribution to anti-Semitism is legend. Tomás de Torquemada, engineer of the Spanish Inquisition, was also a strong after-life believer. Perhaps those are the kinds of "contributions" Lewis so admired.

What about reform Jews and non-believers who have contributed so much to this world that their names would fill volumes, they who never held belief in the afterlife? How does that reconcile with being "ineffective" in this world with no belief in the next? Is it only those Christians who have a weak belief or no belief in an afterlife that are ineffective in this world— all other flavors of believers and non-believers being unaffected in their contributions by their rejection of the afterlife myth? Please.

Yet Christians elevate CS Lewis to cult-figure status, an articulate icon of Christian "Truth," the poster boy for defender of the faith, a man of letters who has tasted the bitterness of godlessness, rejected it, and come back into the light of Jesus' goodness. In reality, Lewis was a religious hack playing to an audience who are as willing to swallow his shallow apologetics whole as it is to accept without question virgin births or dead things coming to life.

Apparently it doesn't take much to be the literary and apologetic hero of Christians. Just say you were an atheist once then blow smoke up their collective asses.

81

God Does Rehab: Seeks to Save Image and Fan Base

01 Sep 2010

Rehab: the last stop before the slammer or complete rejection by the public for so many of today's celebrities who live lives of gross excess, with anger issues, and self-indulgence. As followers and fans drift away from worshipping him, it was just a matter of time before the Judeo-Christian God (aka, "I Am," aka, "Yahweh," aka, "G-D") finally broke down and saw the handwriting on the wall.

I had the opportunity to interview God just before he entered Behavioral Health of the Palm Beaches, Inc. rehab center. The following is a verbatim transcript of our conversation, albeit some of his most vicious epithets and rants have been redacted to spare the sensibilities of my gentle readers.

Hump: Before we start, is it okay if I just call you God?

God: I don't give a Babylonian baby's crushed skull what you call me, as long as you don't call me late for genocide.

Hump: Ah! A not-so-thinly veiled reference to Psalms 137:9, I take it.

God: Oh, you're one of my readers, eh? I suppose you want me to autograph your copy.

Hump: Yes, I've read your work and, no, no autograph required. I just wanted to ask you about committing yourself to rehab. I hear it's about your anger issues.

God: Oh, that. Yeah, my PR folks thought it might be a good idea. They say a few weeks in anger management rehab would be good for my image. Frankly, it's all angel shit.

Hump: You don't sound so committed to the idea. I mean, let's face it: your anger has been documented for some time...like thirty-five hundred years.

God: It's all been blown out of proportion by the media. Those heathen scum will do anything to make me look bad.

Hump: Well, most of what they attribute to you is in your own book. You know, destroying almost every living thing and everyone with a flood, killing the firstborn of Egypt, massacring non-Hebrew tribes down to the last child, demanding people be stoned to death for this and that ...lots of other stuff.

God: Hey, fuck you! That was the old me. Once I became schizophrenic and developed my Jesus personality, I was cool...everybody knows that!

Hump: So they say. But Jesus/You said he came to set father against son, mother against daughter; that he/you didn't come to bring peace; that when he/you return, it will be with a sword in your mouth; and then there's that condemning good folks to eternal torture for not believing in you thing...

God: Yeah, yeah, yeah...spare me the lecture, Sugar Tits.

Hump: Sugar tits?!

God: I picked that up from Mel Gibson, one of my most devoted followers. Catchy, huh? Anyway, he went to rehab for his anger issues so my people figure if I do it and appear contrite, appear to turn over a new leaf, so to speak, maybe not so many of my believers will be abandoning ship. I've been having a few problems filling the pews lately.

Hump: Wouldn't it be more effective if you appeared in the sky over every nation on Earth simultaneously? You could tell folks you're sorry for all the bad stuff you did, that you won't send them to this hell place you created for them...just pedophile ministers and priests, those that protected them, evangelical ministers and faith healers, Fred Phelps, and mass murderers. You can admit that it wasn't anyone's fault but your own that people didn't believe in you, that it's all cool if folks decide they prefer not to worship you.

God: Are you fuckin' nuts? If I did that what would be the point of being a Supreme Being? I might as well tell old peanut breath Ganesh or that doper Vishnu they can take over as my successor. Fuck, no! I didn't spend six days creating the universe and an eternity developing my image just to wimp out of a tried and true fear strategy.

Hump: So, this rehab thing is pretty much a total sham, just like when Mel, Ted Haggard, or Lindsay Lohan checked in?

God: Sham? [chuckling] Is the pope a pedophile-enabling ex-Nazi? Of course it's a sham! But "sham" is such a harsh word. I prefer "act" of God. Get it? Act/ acting? By the way, you put that in print and when I get out of rehab, I'll create a new incurable childhood disease in your name. Maybe you'd like to see a few million third-world babies born with humps on their backs or deformed kidneys.

Hump: You'd do that to innocent children? Just to punish me?

God: What part of my book didn't you understand? Now, fuck off—here comes my driver. I've got a quarter-to-four full-body massage at the rehab and I'm expecting a "happy ending," if you catch my drift.

82

Let There Be Hell on Earth

11 Sep 2010

Nine years ago today, a cell of Muslim fanatics flew airplanes into buildings in New York City and Washington, D.C., and into the ground in Pennsylvania. Nearly three thousand Americans were consumed in the flames of a man-made hell. While a singular event that Americans will never, should never, forget, creating hell on Earth has been the trademark of religionists for millennia. Fire is the stock and trade of religionists.

Some of the earliest pagan religions burned their human victims alive. A super-heated bronze statue of the god Moloch (aka, Molech) was used by his adherents to burn alive selected firstborn infants each year to bring good crops and ensure fertility of the people. Mercifully, drums were beaten so the cries of the infants were drowned out and the parents of the sacrificed didn't have to hear their children's screams of pain.

Fire was the element of choice during the Spanish Inquisition to force confessions from heretics. It was used to slowly roast the Templars, Cathars, Jewish convert backsliders, Christian dissidents, and enemies of the faith, real, perceived, or invented.

The pogroms of Christian anti-Semites throughout Germany, Russia, and Eastern Europe found fire to be an effective cleansing agent when applied liberally to Jewish villages and ghetto enclaves.

For five centuries, the screams of men and women declared witches by the faithful reverberated across Europe and colonial America as flames charred their flesh. It continues to this day as Africans embrace Christian tradition, abide by God's words in Exodus 22:18, and seek out their own witches to roast.

Whenever an insult to their imaginary God or pedophile prophet is perceived, Muslims the world over flick their Bics to burn American and Israeli flags, private property, and effigies.

Devout Christians in the South after the Civil War found that a wooden cross soaked in a flammable substance and burned at night on the property of targeted blacks and Jews was, and still is, an effective terrorist tactic. Plus, it casts a lovely light upon the lynched.

Christians discovered early on that at four hundred and fifty-one degrees Fahrenheit, the books that challenged Christian doctrine, offered alternative answers to "biblical science," entertained children with tales of make-believe wizards, or were otherwise deemed evil or offensive to God and his devoted minions burned rather nicely. Sometimes the volume was chained to the leg of its author before both were reduced to ashes. Fortunately, plastics melt at a slightly lower temperature, making the burning of cassette tapes, vinyl records, CDs, and DVDs much easier for today's zealous faithful to exercise their flaming rituals.

Yes, religionists have always been drawn to fire like mindless moths. Christians say fire represents purity and light and is a symbol of the Holy Spirit. Funny how at the same time fire is the torture method of choice in that mythical, horrific place their God invented to punish non-believers for an eternity. What's not funny or mythical is the reality that religionists have been causing hell on Earth for centuries, with no end in sight. For as long as religions exist the inferno will rage on.

If a Satan existed, he would probably be carrying a cross or a Koran, quoting scripture, claiming the exclusive "Truth," and using flame to underscore his devotion. To paraphrase Pogo, an old comic strip: "Religionists have met Satan... and he is them."

83

The Hideous Grind of Life—The Wondrous Effect of Faith

21 Sep 2010

Last week I received the following message from a reader asking my assistance in responding to a Christian's platitude:

"A Catholic high school classmate of mine posted this. How would you counter it? *'The only way to find happiness in the grind of life is by faith. A faith-filled life means all the difference in how we view everything around us. It affects our attitudes toward people, toward circumstances, toward ourselves. Only then do our feet become swift to do what is right.'*"

My reply follows:

It's unfortunate that some people are so shallow, their lives so unfulfilling, their grasp on reality so loose. Theist willingness to surrender to faith in their imaginary being any personal responsibility for their own condition, morality, and ethics is part and parcel to religion-think and that is precisely what that childlike testimony of your friend expresses. That he disparages life as a "grind" as opposed to a marvelous and wonderful opportunity, an experience to be savored and enjoyed to its fullest all by itself, is the mindset of so many Christians whose pained existence and/or whose perspective of life as being just God's waiting room cause them to seek refuge in the fantasy realm of religion.

Did Mother Teresa's faith influence her "attitude toward people"? Indeed it did. And it caused her to glorify the pain of her patients as a glory to God, *a blessing.* As a result, she withheld pain medication that would have eased the misery of her patients in their final weeks, days, and hours, in spite of the millions of dollars her order amassed. Somehow I don't see that as a good "attitude toward people," or doing what is right by any measure of reasoned thinking. Your friend will likely rationalize Mother Teresa's attitude to have been a wonderful thing, for such is the effect of faith on the mind.

A "faith-filled life" affects how religionists view everything. Some faithful view the unnecessary death of a child caused by parents withholding medication in favor of prayer as "God's Will." Other faith filled lives view competing religions as being from the Devil, and provoke hatred and inspire terror by mindless acts on behalf of their faith. Others fan the spread of AIDS among third-world peoples by rejecting the effectiveness of condoms and the reality of the human sex drive. Still more reject scientific evidence and proofs of the natural world—opting to pass along fabled faith-filled foolishness to their children, stunting their intellectual growth.

Faith causes some people to fly airplanes into buildings, blow up clinics, discriminate against their fellow human beings for their sexual preference, mutilate genitals, kill apostates, justify sexism, disparage all other beliefs or lack thereof because THEIR faith is the "true" faith and the only way to properly live and die.

Yes, sadly it takes the faith-driven expectation of a supernatural reward for them to be moved to "do what is right." That or their "doing what's right" is motivated by their proselytizing agenda. Their sense of right is not out of pure empathy, compassion, and humanity. To them doing right can't co-exist with non-belief because what would be the point. It would be like working without pay.

The fact that empathy exists in all humans, save sociopaths, is lost on them. Only when their minds are willingly vacated of all personal responsibility and the void filled by make-believe do their "feet become swift" to do the right thing. Even then their definition of doing the right thing as often as not means praying, lending neither a helping hand nor financial support to victims' relief.

We, the thinking, can do what's right, and we do... no faith required. We can enjoy life to its fullest and experience happiness, and we do...no faith required. We do so without the fallacy of afterlife rewards or threats, without the mind-numbing drug of religious delusion, and without attributing our charity, happiness, and personal success to a boogie man or a 1st century dead Jew.

The ignorance of faith is indeed bliss to them. They cannot see beyond what they have been programmed to see and that never included questioning their belief, or observing the real world.

84

One Nation, under Jesus, with Liberty and Justice for All Christians

26 Sep 2010

"*A new nationwide umbrella non-profit organization dedicated to restoring our Nation to the original Christian values so that the silencing of Christians will no longer be politically correct.*"

"*Christian Nation Foundation will reclaim and restore our nation's Christian heritage and values by acting as an umbrella organization for all like-minded Americans of all faiths in the cultural war against secular progressives.*"

"*Christian Nation PAC, a political action committee, will bring the necessary and persuasive action so that no one will ever believe America is in a post-Christian era.*"

The above is an extract from Christian Nation (http://christiannation.org/).

While they claim they do not seek to make Christianity the state religion, somehow I'm not reassured, especially since they have decided to ignore and distort historical fact and use rhetoric that would lead the unknowing (or easily led) to believe Christianity is a put-upon minority in jeopardy of being eradicated in the US. If only it were so.

A Google search for "Christian nation" reveals thousands of Christian-nation-endorsing sites, blogs, and religio-political pundits' perspectives. Even the Catholics, who by certain Protestant sect standards aren't even true Christians, get into the act: *"Our constitutional legal system is still based on the Jewish/Christian Bible, not the Koran or other holy book"* (http://www.catholiceducation.org/articles/politics/pg0040.html).

They offer no support for that assertion. How could they, since there is none?

Why should we care about this Christian Nation issue? After all, it's those Muslims who are seeking to "Islamize" America, right? Here's why:

"Sixty-five percent of Americans believe that the nation's founders intended the U.S. to be a Christian nation and 55% believe that the Constitution establishes a Christian nation, according to the 'State of the First Amendment 2007' national survey released Sept. 11 [2007] by the First Amendment Center" (http://www.firstamendmentcenter.org/news.aspx?id=19031).

It's not just a handful of extremists like Hannity, Beck, Palin, and a few Bible Belt congressmen. <u>Sixty-five percent!</u> That's one hundred and ninety-five million Americans who are confused, misguided, uneducated, or just plain wrongheaded.

In comparison, even if 100 percent of Muslims in the US wanted Shariah law, or were hell-bent on converting America to Islam, they would represent only 2.5 million people, less than 1 percent of the population of the US. Leads one to have second thoughts as to who is the greater threat to our freedoms.

Fanatic and ignorant religionists with an agenda are dangerous, no matter what prophet or man-god they follow or worship. We must be on guard against them in any form. But with the growth of secularism in this country, with the newfound courage and openness of atheists to challenge religious intrusion into our lives and government, with our unwillingness to accept the role of second-class citizens, Christians are becoming scared.

They are scared that their delusion is being marginalized. They are scared that people who once were satisfied hiding in the closet to avoid persecution are gaining equal rights, equal status with "normal folk." They are scared that the rejection of archaic, male-dominated biblical prohibitions and antiquated myths will cause Christianity as they know it to be discarded on the giant trash heap of rejected religious doctrine.

That fear is manifesting itself in a resurgence of Christian nationalism, Christian non-think, Christian propaganda, and history revisionism that shows no sign of abating. I expect it to get worse. Turn a blind eye to it at your peril. If you aren't already a paying member of the Freedom from Religion Foundation and Americans United for the Separation of Church and State then repeat after me: "...one nation, under Jesus, with liberty and justice for all Christians."

85

Breaking the "Promoting Family Values" Code

03 Oct 2010

Mrs. Hump and I were watching the morning news when a new car dealership commercial came on. Since car and furniture commercials are all we seem to get here, having a new one to start our day wasn't a real attention-grabber. That is, until I heard the dealer proudly announce the fact that their dealership was *"built on family values."*

"Built on family values?" The term itself is something of an enigma. I'm not privy to what the precise definition is and I certainly haven't the vaguest idea how a car business can be "built" on family values. Whatever its meaning, apparently it is understood only by those to whom the term "family values" is like a secret handshake, a code word, a wink and a nod to some shared doctrine.

Over the past twenty-five years or so, Evangelicals/the ultra-conservative Christian right seem to have developed the term to identify who is with 'em and who is agin 'em. Evidently, folks like defrocked Rev. Ted Haggard, soon-to-be-defrocked Bishop Eddie Long, thrice-married Newt Gingrich, playboy Rep. Mark Souder (R-Indiana), airport men's room limbo king Larry Craig (R-Idaho), prescription druggie Rush Limbaugh, and the pedophile-protecting pope all endorse and promote family values. Meanwhile, people like Barney Frank (D-MA), Ellen DeGeneres, President Obama, Christopher Hitchens, and everyone who opposes religion in the government or supports equal rights for non-believers, gays, and a women's right to choose are intent on devaluing if not destroying families / family values.

I'm used to seeing the term applied liberally in campaign ads run by Republican candidates. Apparently the passing of the health care bill, the recession, the unemployment rate, illegal aliens, the 9/11 attacks, hurricanes, and floods are all attributable to the erosion of family values. Who knew?

I hear the term drip from the greasy lips of evangelical preachers and post-polygamy Mormons who have no problem crossing the line of Church and State separation and investing church millions trying to overturn laws in states in which they don't even reside.

From what I can determine, the rise of atheism, decline of religiosity, push toward stem-cell research, acceptance of evolutionary theory, inoculating children against polio, use of birth control, aborting a fetus that was the product of rape or incest, opposition to the war in Iraq, legalization of gay marriage, and rampant unrestrained masturbation have contributed to the demise of family values. Is it any wonder Christian families are divorcing in record numbers?

What the family values proponents agenda has to do with your family, my family, my son's family, my neighbors' families, or anyone's family can only be conceived in the fevered minds of religionist fanatics. It appears that they perceive any behavior not specifically endorsed by their ancient book of fables as an affront to *their* families' very survival. It seems how they raise and discipline *their* kids, what *they* watch on the tube or view on the Internet, how much quality time *they* spend together, what books *they* read, how strong *their* marriage is, are somehow degraded, devalued, and negatively impacted by those of us who do not share their politics, religious precepts, sexual practices, or their concept of "family values."

I expect the family values hypocrisy mania to remain the war cry of Christian theocrats and conservative fear-mongers for years to come. That it has now become a business marketing tool, however, comes as a complete surprise. How long before *"Our chickens were raised with family values"* becomes a KFC motto to get the God-fearing to eat more of their buckets of deep-fried fowl?

The next time that car dealership commercial airs, I'm going to catch its name and send them an email. I'll ask, if their dealership was built on family values, does that mean they don't want contraceptive-using couples, pro-choice advocates, atheists, gay and women's rights advocates, or masturbators as clients lest it undermine their family's longevity or company's stability. After all, I'd hate to make a trip down there for nothing.

86

The Thing behind the Curtain

13 Oct 2010

L eave reality behind for a moment and allow yourself a flight of fantasy.

Imagine that the president of the United States, arguably the most powerful man on the planet, has never been seen. He never ran for office and was never elected by official ballot. No one has ever personally met him. He never meets with foreign officials. He never speaks publicly. He never appears in person, in pictures, or on TV, the radio, or the Internet. He is said to have written or at least "inspired" a book to be written that defines his political positions and vision for the nation, albeit the original text has never been seen; only redacted and reshuffled copies of the original manuscript exist.

Instead of having just one press secretary to interpret his book of policies, issue his edicts, explain his positions, and define his objectives, he has thousands upon thousands of self-appointed spokesmen-spin doctors speaking on his behalf. Many if not most of their interpretations and explanations are in diametric opposition to some of their fellow spokesmen's understandings and pronouncements. Each of them accuses the other of being false spokesmen, or "not true press secretaries."

The result could best be described as chaos. It wouldn't take long for the American public to become disillusioned and completely dismissive of the nation's leader and his self-appointed, quasi-official mouthpieces. Surely calls for impeachment would follow; people would be on the verge of revolution; the heads of the soothsayer spokesmen would roll in the streets. Shouts of *"Mr. President, show yourself and speak to us directly! Prove you are who your spin doctors say you are, or which one they say you are, if you 'are' at all! Resolve the confusion and conflicts among your official un-official professors once and for all!"* would resound from every media outlet in the nation.

Absurd, you say? Who could imagine such a thing, or allow it to happen? How could anyone give that president or his "ministers of spin" any credibility, much less entrust him or them to guide their lives for even a moment, much less a four- or eight-year term? It's beyond imagination, simply implausible.

And yet the vast majority of Americans and billions of people around the world not only endure such a construct, they endorse it, couldn't conceive of existence any other way. Not just for four or eight years, but for their entire lives. Just substitute the word "God" for the title "president," and "clergy" for his thousands of press secretary minions, and what I described in my hypothetical construct becomes as real and as natural as a priest's erection at a choirboys' rehearsal.

One would think (if one can think at all) that when your invisible and silent divine being needs an army of contradicting spokesmen, all of whom claim to be speaking for it, you can pretty much figure the reclusive and inscrutable divine thing they profess to speak for is either senile and confused, mute and in a coma, or non-existent.

Instead, the faithful take sides. They form into competing parties that proclaim THEIRS to be the one true "party of God"; THEIR spokesman best represents THEIR God's/gods' wishes. THEY represent the true invisible silent God. By default, the others worship a false invisible silent god and follow the interpretation of a false or deceived prophet/not a true believer-spokesman.

Sound crazy? It is. It's the stuff of fantasy stories like *Alice in Wonderland, The Wizard of Oz,* or *Gulliver's Travels.* Stories that, if they were real places with real people, would be a nightmarish existence where fiction is taken as fact, lies accepted as truth, confusion and contradiction perceived as clarity and cohesion, edicts of genocide and violent punishment perceived as just, good, and loving.

If forced to live in such a world, I would do what I do now—use every opportunity to proclaim: *"Pay no attention to the thing behind the curtain. It does not exist; and the ones speaking for it in front of the curtain are full of shit."*

87

The Invocation

19 Oct 2010

Whether at a graduation ceremony or some solemn public gathering, it's not uncommon for a clergyman to be invited to deliver an invocation to launch the event. Although they may exist, I have yet to hear one that is anything more than the shaman calling upon a magical spirit to bless the assembly and otherwise invoke its supernatural guidance.

Invocations sometimes precede governmental sessions. While they are supposed to be generic, the occasional fanatical pulpiteer will thrust his preferred deity's name into the script in violation of the First Amendment's prohibition of the endorsement of a specific religion by the government. The fact that some of the attendees don't recognize said deity and find it exclusionary, or even offensive, is not recognized by the Bible-thumper. Or (and this is more likely) the sky pilot couldn't care less if it irks some because he sees it as his divinely directed duty to shove his God down people's throats, welcome or not.

Of course, if the invocation is delivered by a pagan (aka, non-Abrahamic religionist, which happens about as frequently as Halley's Comet, albeit far too often if you ask the followers of the predominant faith) and the deity mentioned happens to be one with four arms and an elephant's trunk, you can be assured the howls of disgust and cries of *"blasphemy!"* would be deafening. This is never perceived as hypocrisy by the offended shepherds or sheep of the one "true" faith.

This sectarian tradition isn't disappearing any time soon in the US. It would be political suicide for a public official to come out against religious invocations. In the meantime freethinker watchdog organizations have been bringing suits when citizens of standing have brought these violations to their attention. But this doesn't mean religionists have to own the right to deliver invocations at public events. Atheist activists have the opportunity, the duty, to get onboard the invocation bandwagon.

What would an atheist's invocation sound like? How about an appeal to reason, a wish for respect for attendees' opposing positions, an imploration for community, civility, compromise, goodwill, empathy, and reasoned discussion? All of those things are grounded in realism and foundational to productive discourse. It's what the thinking in an advanced society do.

I was asked by a friend to compose a pre-dinner invocation for his family's Thanksgiving gathering. The gathering includes both believers and non-believers and for once he'd like to share a thought that isn't religiously inspired. I offered him this:

It is an American tradition that on the fourth Thursday in November family and friends gather together to give thanks for the bounty we enjoy as a free people. It is proper that we should.

Our thanks belong to the brave men and women who founded this nation on principles of common law, reason, and morality that have evolved over time to ensure the continuity of society and deliver the best possible well-being for everyone who is willing to work for it. No demands for obedience to some disembodied power, no threats of retribution for freethinking, no mandated kowtowing to any man or myth.

We are gathered here to thank our Founding Fathers for their foresight, to enjoy the warmth and love of family and friends, and to offer them our thanks for making our lives fuller and happier.

A toast to our forefathers, to those who have given so much to keep America free, to America, to reason, to good will, and to our lasting health, love and happiness.

A word of advice: If invited to speak at an event other than an all atheist gathering, you'll want to suppress the urge to blurt out, "*Thanks for coming. I have no supernatural horse hockey to feed you as though you are a herd of mindless medieval peasants. I have too much respect for your intellect. So, let's get on with reality and the event.*" After all, you'll want to be invited back, hopefully before Halley's Comet's next appearance.

88

Close Encounters of the Religious Kind

24 Oct 2010

I was startled when I opened the door and found Kdlgr standing there, mouth agape and breathing hard. I hadn't expected to see him back so soon, but there he was: beady-eyed, a viscous slime dripping from his pie hole, his Rastafarian-like head tendrils all askew, worked up and on the verge of hysteria.

"Kdlgr, you look terrible...what the heck happened?" I asked. "Hump, dude...I need a drink. Can I come in?" he rasped and clicked through clinched fangs.

I held the door wide. He ducked down and made his way to the living room, his green reptilian-scaled, eight-foot-tall frame collapsing hard into the brown leather recliner. I grabbed the bottle of Jack Daniels from the liquor cabinet and poured him a flower vase full, neat, just the way I knew he liked it. He slurped it down. I handed him the bottle. I figured it best to let him finish a second drink before I started to quiz him. He was a frightful mess.

I met Kdlgr in the fall of last year. He had just arrived on Earth and had an unfortunate incident with one of those three-hundred-foot-tall windmills recently erected the next town over. Four miles and seven minutes later, I had a house guest. He was dripping a nasty-looking fluid from a gash in his thorax.

Mrs. Hump and I patched him up. He explained that he was a respected social scientist on his planet. His mission was to become familiar with Earth culture. The approach: to blend in, become as inconspicuous as possible, and meet as many humans as he could on a one-on-one basis, all the while keeping as low a profile as a giant reptile can.

As I had expected, that wasn't working for him.

His eyes were a little glazed now and his breathing more controlled but still labored. He took another long gulp of Jack and started spilling his guts…figuratively, this time.

"Hump, it was horrible," he croaked.

"Start from the beginning, and slowly," I replied.

He took a deep breath. "So I was in disguise, you know…the trench coat and fake beard you lent me. Your people hardly gave me a second glance. I made my way down the East Coast—places Mapquest calls Massachusetts, Connecticut, New York, New Jersey. Oh, by the way, New Jersey smells like the sphincter of a Galeneese dipdophoil worm." I nodded in concurrence.

"Anyway, things were going fine. I met many intelligent humans, gathered much data about your culture, history, scientific advancements, and what you call fornicating. Then I made my way to a place called Missishitty."

"Uh, that's Mississippi," I corrected him.

"Yes, Mississippi. I came across this white building, walked in, and sat among the occupants. They had their eyes closed and were waving their arms in the air while some guy with white puffy hair urged them on. I couldn't understand what they were saying. Their language was like a hybrid of Hycatefic and gutter Romelian but made less sense. Next thing you know they were flopping to the floor, falling over each other. I was scared there was a radiation leak in my beaferl pack, it was that bad."

"Ah! Okay, they are Pentecostals. It's a Christian religious sect," I explained, recognizing the bizarre antics.

"Yeah, whatever." He dismissed my interruption and went on, stopping just long enough to finish the third vase of Jack. "I was scared, and got up to leave. But before I could get out they surrounded me, making these weird sounds. One of them told me about this god thing, that it created life on your planet in the past six thousand years, that it made all humans in its image." He paused. "No offense, Hump, but this god must be one ugly motherfucker." I nodded.

"The guy with the white puffy hair and gold chains told me about how this god tortured his own offspring to death and that he did it for ME! That freaked me out. And then things started to get really bad, Hump. Next thing you know they ripped off my trench coat and attempted to take my pressurized suit off. I wasn't about to show my bindlegh to a bunch of crazed Earthlings. When I tried to stop them, they grabbed me and carried me over to this pool of H_2O and were about to throw me in, mumbling something about washing away my sins."

I winced. Mrs. Hump and I found out the hard way last year when we attempted to wash Kdlgr's wounds that H_2O is to him what sulfuric acid is to human flesh.

"Jesus Christ, then what happened?" I blurted out.

"DON'T USE THAT NAME...IT SCARES THE PDLKT OUT OF ME," he roared back, almost jumping out of the chair.

He went on. "Well, I did the only thing I could think of at the time. I mean, my very essence was at stake. Honest, Hump, I couldn't think of anything else to do," he stammered, sounding like a guilty kid ready to confess to sticking a firecracker up a frog's ass.

"What? What did you do, Kdlgr?" I cringed and waited for the shoe to drop.

"The unthinkable, Hump, the unthinkable!!! I killed them all and ate their carbon-based life forms," he blurted out.

I fell back into my chair, took a long draught from my Grey Goose martini with three olives, and let out a deep sigh. "Whew, Kdlgr, you scared the shit outta me. For a second there I thought you were going to tell me you converted."

Talk about close encounters.

89

Quandary over US Catholic Attrition? Maybe They Should Ask an Atheist

04 Nov 2010

The *National Catholic Reporter* reports that *"…Catholicism is experiencing the largest loss of faithful of any religious denomination in America"* (http://ncronline.org/blogs/ncr-today/had-it-catholics-part-ii?nocache=1#comment-161935).

The reason for this decline seems to elude the Catholic hierarchy. Could that be the same hierarchy that still believes in demonic possession? Go figure.

While the Catholic leadership seems to be bamboozled by this and spends their time gnashing their teeth and wringing their hands over the exodus of the faithful, as an atheist I am able to better see the forest for the trees. Why are they losing membership in America in spite of the influx of Hispanic immigrants who are overwhelmingly Catholic? Let me count the ways:

1. The Church's inane position on contraception: The pope's claim that condoms contribute to AIDS is proof of blatant denial of reality and scientific truth.

Meanwhile, uncontrolled birth rates in third-world countries are sucking their resources dry, a recipe for global disaster. In thirty years the population of the planet is expected to double. Where will the already scarce water necessary for this population explosion's existence come from? Continuing this absurd stance is tantamount to endorsing environmental and social disaster and the wholesale spread of famine and disease.

2. An unnatural fixation with genitalia: Whose penis is going into whom? What rights do women have over their own uterus? The condemnation of masturbation. The insistence on celibacy for priests. Declaring homosexuality to be a crime against God and an individual choice. It's time to acknowledge that sex is part of life, part of the natural world, and not subject to supernaturalist control or dictates by men who use their penis only for urination...or are supposed to.

3. Institutionalized hypocrisy: Not a single Nazi was ever ex-communicated for their murder of six million Jews, yet the Church ex-communicates nuns who support women in the priesthood, or who report priestly misconduct. They threaten ex-communication for Catholic politicians who support a woman's right to choose. Is this "God's justice"? It certainly isn't Man's.

Clergy wear gold-threaded dresses trimmed in ermine and jewel-encrusted hats that look like a psychotic went wild with a Bedazzler; carry gold chalices, and solid gold crosses all while people shell out money to the Church they can ill afford to give up. Christ would be spinning in his grave over such finery, if he ever existed. Perhaps the Church had forgotten that Jesus said to his apostles when he sent them out to preach the Word: "*Take nothing for your journey, no staff, nor bag, nor bread, nor money—not even an extra tunic*"

(Luke 9:3). What's wrong with this picture could be discerned by a reasonably astute twelve-year-old.

Meanwhile, as I write this, the Vatican's bank is being investigated by Italian courts for money-laundering. Already, the authorities have seized thirty million dollars of the Vatican bank's funds (http://www.google.com/hostednews/canadianpress/article/ALeqM5hHVTPs_OJiq1vPlrewQfWJeSG9xA?docId=4915482).

4. Enabling of molesting priests: Cover-ups and insufficient action against those who perpetrated it or enabled it. Not a single ex-communication for sexual misconduct or Church subterfuge to date. Not one powerful action that would purge those suspected of being perverts or prevent the ordination of them. Again, as I write this, ten thousand pages of previously secret documents have been discovered that prove the diocese of San Diego, California, intentionally covered up known molestations by priests and transferred them to other dioceses (http://www.washingtonpost.com/wp-dyn/content/article/2010/10/24/AR2010102401721.html?wprss=rss_religion/wires).

5. Superstitious nonsense: The gross foolishness of transubstantiation, of exorcism/demonic possession, of bleeding statues and supernaturally empowered relics and bones, of miracles old and new. Only the weakest minds, the hardcore unquestioning, the core of the Church's mostly aged faithful still buy it. Educated youth are abandoning these absurdities in droves.

6. The politicizing and foolishness of "sainthood": Silly and archaic, it borders on polytheism. Mother Teresa endorsed pain as a glory to God. Is that the behavior of a saint? By whose definition of morality?

A patient prays to another obscure dead nun, experiences cancer remission (while on chemotherapy and radiation, by the way), and suddenly the dead nun is working miracles and ready to be given goddess-like status.

Pope John Paul II is being credited with healing a nun with Parkinson's disease after she prayed to him. There is no confirmation from medical authorities she ever had the disease. But never mind, John Paul's corpse will be dragged out of the Vatican crypt, his coffin put on display, and fast-tracked to sainthood for his "miracle." Only the most deluded faithful can still possibly believe this claptrap. Is it any wonder why the average age of the dedicated Catholic non-Hispanic church-goer is fifty years old? (http://www.nd.edu/~icl/study_reports/report2.pdf)

The primitive dogma and rituals of Catholicism have become obsolete in the twenty-first century. The time for the Church to adapt to the scientific age and come to reason is way past due. It's time to drop the spooky nuttiness, to abandon the madness of dictating humans' sexual and reproductive behavior, to adjust their focus to more relevant issues of the era and in meaningful ways that directly enhance the lives of people in real-world terms.

Catholic hierarchy, you've been placed on notice—your parishioners are steadily moving toward reality, your best efforts to stem that tide not withstanding. Now you know why.

Of course, all this will be wasted on those who have made careers as professional purveyors of superstition, go-betweens to a make-believe spirit and the religiously infected. But who cares? Whether they adapt to a more reasoned modernist approach to morality and the issues important to human well-being, or choose to remain mired in ancient ignorance and irrelevance—it's all good.

Their losses are our gain.

90

Probability or Purpose? How Will Your Religious Friends Explain This?

13 Nov 2010

Zahra Baker was a ten-year-old girl from North Carolina. Her parents divorced; her father had custody. A bone cancer survivor, she had her leg amputated and lost part of her hearing as a side effect but by all accounts was a happy and well-adjusted little girl. Missing for weeks, her prosthetic leg and part of her remains were discovered not far from her home. Her stepmother, who admitted writing a fake ransom note, is now the primary suspect in her murder, possibly aided by the child's father.

I heard this report for the first time this morning. I was appalled that so much sorrow, pain, and horror could be condensed into the ten short years of that child's life.

As a realist, I understand it, however. Divorce is rampant, with almost 50 percent of marriages ending in separation. Childhood cancer is a fact of life affecting approximately two out of every ten thousand children in the US each year, roughly 0.02 percent of children. The horrific acts of abuse and violence against children, while inexplicable to most of us, are an unfortunate reality. The murder of children under the age of fifteen represents approximately thirteen hundred/ 6 percent of US murders annually. A child has approximately 0.00014 percent chance of being murdered.

The odds of any one child experiencing what Zahra Baker went through are beyond my ability to calculate. To say they are remote is an understatement. Sadly, Zahra was the loser in a trifecta of astronomical statistical improbably. But that is exactly what it was.

So how do religionists explain this? Can they dismiss this as a horrific statistical reality stemming from a convergence of random natural occurrences? No… they cannot. Not even if they want to. According to doctrine, their God has a "purpose" for every person. Their loving God, who watches over his creations with unlimited beneficence—a God who answers the prayers of believers—doesn't play with random statistics. Everything is by design, even Zahra's miserable life and horrific death.

What will your Xtian friends and relatives say if you were to ask them what God's purpose was for this little girl's birth, suffering, and violent early death? There aren't a lot of options from which they can choose. While apologists have written several million words trying to explain away why their God permits these things to happen to innocents, it always boils down to the vapid platitudes that believers have adopted in lieu of thought to avoid coming to grips with reality. So, here are the choices:

"God works in strange and mysterious ways."

"It's all part of God's plan…who are we to understand it?"

"God needed her in heaven."

"God wanted her to experience the ultimate pain in order to appreciate the ultimate happiness."

"She's in a better place."

Perhaps one will invoke the ever-handy *"free will,"* whatever the hell that means. Sometimes they will dig really deep and proffer that *"God is a good and loving God,"* as though that explains/excuses it all. That it doesn't explain anything doesn't get a second thought.

Want to know how deeply your most devout theist friends have bought into unquestioning religious non-think? Want to gauge exactly how all-encompassing is their surrender to vacuous apologetics and religious gibberish? Want to witness what complete abandonment of reality sounds like? Ask them to explain God's purpose for Zahra Baker, then stand back and watch the dance of denial. If one of them invokes "probability," give them this book. They are on the cusp of reality.

91

"We Need an Atheist Church": Here We Go Again

18 Nov 2010

Well, it's happened again. I was surfing the net and found an atheist site that was taking a poll of its membership, asking if they'd approve of and attend an atheist "church." I was disgusted for a number of reasons.

First, the term "church" is antithetical to atheism. A church is a place of worship, for theists (http://diction-ary.reference.com/browse/church). They might have just as well proffered an atheist synagogue, or mosque, or coven for all the sense it makes.

Secondly, with so many confused theists calling atheism a religion, and all the atheists working to counter that foolishness by repeating the old canards like "atheism is a religion like baldness is a hair color," or "like NOT collecting stamps is a hobby," to be talking about an "atheist church" is giving already confused theists ammunition to renew their claim of atheism = religion.

Thirdly, exactly what do all atheists have in common to justify a close-knit social structure akin to a theist congregation? Do we all share a "belief system" in common, or a common worldview? I doubt it. You don't know mine, I don't know yours, and nothing about being atheist defines one's wider personal convictions or worldview.

Do we feel the need for some "spiritual support" (oy!) by a group of like-minded non-believers? Thanks, but reality is all the support I need. Atheists share in common only one thing, the *only* thing meant by atheism: non-belief in God/gods. We share no rituals, dogma, doctrine, rites, or even a secret handshake. Frankly, I wouldn't even be interested in attending a night of bingo with a room full of atheists.

Oh, yes, many of us share some basic axiomatic principles, like respect for science and the need for objective evidence to accept something as a fact. Most of us accept evolutionary theory as genuine. Some large percentage of us supports equality for women, a woman's right to control her reproductive processes, and gay rights. But that isn't atheism. That's modernity, rationality, and respect for freedom.

The concept of a church that seeks to somehow service my needs (whatever they may be) or the needs of the "atheist community" (whatever that is), simply because we share only non-belief in God/gods, is not only unnecessary but irrational and counterproductive to how freethinkers are perceived.

That's not to say I object to atheist clubs, reading groups, discussion forums, or activist organizations to discuss issues, raise awareness, and to ensure that atheists' rights and the separation of Church and State are kept sacrosanct. I belong to a number of those and they serve a clear and defined purpose, none of them "spiritual." But the concept of a formalized "church" is downright misguided, oxymoronic, and sets back the hard-won credibility of the atheist movement twenty-five years.

On the other hand, if by calling every atheist organization a church, mosque, synagogue, or coven we all get a major tax break...count me in and call me "Reverend."

92

Prayer Requests: The Desperation of the Deluded

24 Nov 2010

I stumbled across a website that encourages Christians to submit their prayer requests. They promise that the faithful will take up their cause and help them petition God for redress. On a whim, I searched "prayer requests" and found thousands of similar sites.

Picking a few of these sites at random, I scrolled through the appeals for prayer requests from hundreds of sad and desperate people. Each story, each testimony, was more pathetic than the one before it. Here are a few extracts:

- *"Lord, I am asking for a husband."*
- *"Dear Jesus, please make a miracle happen for my whole finances and income really soon..."*
- *"Please pray God will rid me of my doubt, fears, disobedience, and replace them with unwavering faith, courage, and willingness to obey God."*

- *"Please pray that my anxiety and panic will leave me. I suffer greatly when I am alone or traveling and I pray that God will make his presence felt... I also pray for a job closer to home to reduce the panic. I pray it is something I love instead of dreading getting up each morning."*
- *"I am falling back into a dpression [sic] again after losing my mom and husabnd [sic] i [sic] have met anew[sic] guy but i [sic] am unsure if he loves me Please pary [sic] to God he is the right one because my lomliness [sic] is unbearable."*

There are literally thousands of these cries for help on just this one site (http://www.urgentprayers.com/).

As I read these prayer requests I was met by three conflicting emotions. First, the realist in me caused my initial response to be one of scorn. How could people possibly believe their financial, relationship, and emotional problems will be solved by typing in appeals to an imaginary God on the Internet and enlisting the prayers of fellow believers? After all, unless their God is senile or illiterate, one prayer request should be sufficient to get its attention and prompt the desired response. If they have prayed and haven't gotten relief, why not just accept "No!" for an answer? Why would a quorum, a veritable petition of prayers, be necessary to get this loving and caring and all-knowing God's attention and get him to respond? Why not conclude the obvious: that there is nothing there listening?

But then the humanist in me replaced that dismissive scorn with sadness and empathy. These are folks who presumably were indoctrinated into supernaturalism through no fault of their own. Whether from childhood, or as a result of weak-minded susceptibility in later life, they have come to believe that they are but helpless pawns in a chess game of life where the pieces are moved by a great unseen spirit's hand. They are merely microscopic cogs in God's great plan. Their own effort, self-determination, and choices are insufficient to influence their life for the better. God's plan guides all and only through his divine intervention can that plan be altered and their life be salvaged. I genuinely pity these people.

Finally, my anti-theism flooded me with anger. Among the prayer sites I perused, not one of them encouraged the prayerful to seek professional attention. Not one of them suggested getting psychiatric help for depression or anxiety, which, through modern pharmaceuticals, could give them almost certain relief. Not one of them recommended secular books that could give them professional self-help guidance. Not one of them directed them to a marriage counselor, financial consultant, career counselor, or grief counselor who could aid them in getting a grasp on their lives and make it a happier existence.

Instead, by their very existence, these sites promote dependency on supernatural intervention which will never come. They discourage affirmative action and self-determination. They prolong the pain of these desperate, deluded folks, some of whom will very likely be destroyed when secular resources could have been their true salvation. These sites are guilty of benign neglect of the very people they call their brothers and sisters in Christ.

For every believer who comes back to testify to Jesus' deliverance from their problem and to thank the site for their type-written prayers, there are likely hundreds who will quietly slip under the waves of hopelessness and drown in despair, dragged down by the weight of religious ignorance. All while the life jacket of secular reality bobs untouched on the surface.

93

"The Vast Majority of Muslims Reject Violence": Let's Define "Vast"

o6 Dec 2010

The violence perpetrated across the globe in the name of Islam and Allah over the past forty years or so is committed by a small percentage of radicals who, we are constantly reminded, distort Muslim values and the words of the Koran. Time and again we are told that the "vast majority" of Muslims are peace-loving people who deplore violence in the name of their religion. To question this is to open oneself up to accusations of "Islamophobe" or "far-right alarmist" by the enlightened politically correct.

I am neither phobic, far-right, nor an alarmist. I'm also not politically correct.

I am, however, skeptical by nature. I require objective evidence before I accept as fact statements posited as true. I am dubious of claims that are repeated so often that, like mindless religious sheep, we are expected to accept them at face/buy into them on faith. I'll leave that kind of non-think to theists. Give me some scientifically gathered supportive data for a claim.

I have long wondered exactly what is meant by "vast majority." I would venture to say that hearing that terminology, most of us would apply single digits, perhaps 2 to 8 percent, to those Muslims who support violence...the "vast majority" of peace-loving Muslims thus being 92 to 98 percent. But in so doing, we'd be grossly mistaken.

The Pew Research Center, one of the world's most highly respected institutes for scientific polling, has issued its latest findings on Muslim attitudes on politics and opinion in seven Muslim nations. Here is a brief synopsis of their findings:

- The median percentage of those surveyed who support the most radical terrorist organization, al Qaeda, is 22 percent, almost one out of four.
- The median percentage for those who support Osama Bin Laden is 21 percent.
- The median percentage of those who support Hezbollah is 35 percent.
- The median percentage of those who support suicide bombing is 20 percent.

Here is the full report: http://pewglobal.org/2010/12/02/muslims-around-the-world-divided-on-hamas-and-hezbollah/.

Given this data, it appears that "vast majority" of peace-loving, anti-terror, anti-extremist Muslims means approximately 65 to 79 percent. Or, to look at it another way, between two and four out of every ten Muslims in these countries endorse the use of violence to promote fanatical Muslim objectives.

To be sure, approximately 75 percent opposing violence is a majority compared to the roughly 25 percent endorsing it. And I'm certainly happy that it's not the reverse. But while 75 vs. 25 percent would be a landslide if we were speaking in terms of election results, when it comes to dismissing Muslim support for fanaticism, violence, death, and hostility against non-Muslims, to use the term "vast majority" is not only a little optimistic, it's an outright distortion.

If 25 percent of Americans, one in four of your neighbors, endorsed the murder of innocents to promote their agenda, or praised Timothy McVeigh, or supported fanatical survivalist groups, or applauded abortion clinic bombing, or felt that blowing oneself up in pursuit of a political or religious goal was justified, I dare say we'd be rather alarmed. But because we are speaking of a specific religion and culture, we are willing to tiptoe and discount the 25 percent as just a "small minority" of that group.

The next time you hear the politically correct, head-in-the-sand apologists downplay the violent nature of Islam, you may want to challenge their understanding of "vast majority" or "small minority." Or you may prefer to ignore scientific fact and rely on blind belief. We know how that works.

94

Taking Atheist Activism to the Extreme: Crossing the Line to Big Brotherism

11 Dec 2010

I don't remember when or why I joined a Facebook cause entitled *Ban Religious Child Grooming*, but evidently I did. I was reminded of this when I received an alert from the cause administrator about some religious event or organization's effort to proselytize children. Clicking on the link, I read the "about us" section for the cause and withdrew from it post haste, hopefully not losing a Facebook friend or two in so doing.

By now I hope my readership has come to know that I am no shrinking violet when it comes to anti-theist activism and calling religious teaching what it is. But there are limits to what I am willing to do to curb the spread of theism.

No one is more aware of the travesty that religious delusion wreaks on civilization. I am well acquainted with the ill effects religious training of children in their formative years has on their acceptance of secular reality, as well as its long-term impact on the propagation of the God Virus. And while I applaud their sensitivity and awareness of the ills of religious indoctrination, advocating banning the teaching of anything—any belief system, presumed fact, unproven theory, conspiracy theory, world view, et al—when it is endorsed and approved by the parent guardian of a minor is a recipe for disaster.

Foundational to the *Ban Religious Child Grooming* credo is this:

- *Only proven fact should ever be taught as being actual facts.*
  [So much for teaching String Theory.]
- *Without religious child grooming the Twin Towers would still be standing.*
  [How could anyone possibly know this? One wonders if that is an actual "fact" or conjecture.]
- *Without religious child grooming thousands of wars would never have occurred.*
  ["Thousands"? Is that a factual statistic? Sounds like an exaggeration, at best.
- *The proven fact of evolution also acts as 100% proof that the biblical accounts of creation are a sham and a deception.*
  [Only if the religionist interprets the creation story literally; if interpreted as a euphemism for natural causes of creation, is it still deception or just a parable?]
- *The age of consent laws and the fraud laws should already be protecting children from religious child grooming, but these crimes are basically ignored.*
  ["Fraud laws"? Would a parent be liable for fraud for proffering Santa, the Easter Bunny, and the Tooth Fairy to their five-year-old? Is

promoting belief in God/gods in and of itself religious child grooming?]

One tends to get on pretty boggy ground when one speaks of "actual fact." Evolutionary theory has already undergone some changes since Darwin's day. It is likely new discoveries will enhance/change our understanding of the "actual facts" of evolution and the Big Bang. Should we ban the teaching of them today because it is more certain than not that what we think we know as fact now will be tweaked or corrected and certain current details of these theories will be proven to be erroneous, thus not "actual fact"?

Last week NASA claimed to have discovered a new life form on Earth: bacteria that live on and reproduce arsenic in place of phosphorous. Turns out this shattering discovery may not be exactly as it was described and is under peer review. If it turns out to be something less factual than declared I wonder what the statute of limitations would be and NASA's penalty.

Once upon a time, the teaching of a solar-centric universe was banned. Proclaiming one's atheism was banned. Reading unpopular books was banned. Practicing certain religions was banned. And not just by religious authority, but by secular governments as well. Banning almost never has the desired effect. All banning achieves is driving the undesired activity underground...the use of illicit drugs and the prominence of prostitution are witness to that.

But beyond this, the slippery slope becomes a cliff. If we empower the government to ban religious teaching of children, irrespective of its degree of absurdity and (potential) negative impact on the child and society, we open the door to banning any new thought or hypothesis or unpopular idea. It is Big Brother at his very ugliest and virulent.

I'm all for aggressive activism, but only when rights and freedoms aren't trashed. To do otherwise makes us exactly what we as thinking people despise: intolerant, short-sighted, unthinking, fanatical, dictatorial, and dangerous.

95

Praise the Lord and Lose the Lard: Jesus Fat Camp May Be Your Kid's Salvation

16 Dec 2010

It's no secret that the US has a major problem with childhood obesity. Thirty percent of our children are overweight or obese. While much lip service has been paid to the issue, one man of God claims to have the ultimate answer.

The Right Reverend Doctor Jackie Butkes runs the Praise Our Redeemer King Youth Kamp and Indoctrination Depot, affectionately referred to by its clients and campers by its acronym, *PORKY KID*. Located in Ft. Myers, Florida, "Porky Kid" promises to bring your chubby youngster closer to God and closer to the weight of a non-porcine species. During Reverend Dr. Butkes' annual recruiting tour of New England, I had the opportunity to interview him with an eye toward finding out the secret to the success of his camp. His only stipulation was no microphones and no notes. So, naturally, I recorded it.

Hump: Reverend, I understand that your camp guarantees significant weight loss through a personal relationship with Jesus. How exactly how do you accomplish that?

Rev. B: Find Jesus!

Hump: Um, sorry, Reverend, I'm not in the market for proselytizing and I'm not sure how that's relevant to...

Rev. B: No, no...that's how we do it. We have the kids *find Jesus!*

Hump: So, sort of a combination of New Testament Bible study and intensive reading of biblical criticism, the transcripts from the Jesus seminar, and various perspectives of the Church's founding fathers to give the children the sense that the power of the Lord will help sustain them through their weight loss crusade?

Rev. B: No. One of our counselors dresses in a beard, sandals, and a diaper, and hides somewhere on our camp grounds. We tell the kids to go find Jesus or they get no food that day.

Hump: That's pretty Machiavellian. You'd think parents would be a little disturbed by that technique.

Rev. B: Nah. The kids don't tell their parents. We tell 'em that if they tell Jesus won't love them, that God will send a pair of bears to tear them apart, and that their parents will die and go directly to hell.

Hump: Seems a little harsh, coercive, and even abusive.

Rev. B: Hey, we guarantee the fat kids will lose weight. This works. If it ain't broke, don't fix it. Jesus said that.

Hump: No, he didn't. But never mind. Is that the whole weight-loss program: hide-and-seek with a fake Jesus?

Rev. B: Not hardly! One of our most effective methods is playing "Wander the Desert or You Get No Dessert." That's where we drive the kids out into the middle of our ten-square-mile compound blindfolded. Then we take off the blindfolds and tell them to find their way back to camp.

Hump: With a counselor and water, I assume.

Rev. B: Did Jesus have a counselor and water with him when he wandered the desert for forty days and forty nights? I don't dang-diddly think so!

Hump: But it's Ft. Myers, Florida. The average daytime temperature in July and August is like ninety degrees with ninety percent humidity!

Rev. B: That's right. We like to give our campers a taste of the Holy Land along with a relationship with Jesus.

Hump: But it's dangerous; kids could die out there!

Rev. B: And they have. It was God's will. We tell their parents that they were Raptured ahead of everyone else because Jesus was so impressed with their sleek new body.

Hump: And the parents believe that???

Rev. B: Of course they do...they're Christians. Believing is what we do. Besides, what's better: having a slim but constantly hungry and whining kid who you know is just gonna get fat again, or having a kid in great shape playing dodge ball with the Lord and hobnobbing with the angels? Plus, the significantly reduced food expense seems to console them.

Hump: Yeah. Uh...well, one last question. What about this promise of a closer relationship with Jesus? Nothing I've heard so far suggests you do much to promote that.

Rev. B: That's 'cause you haven't been to our camp after lights out, and listened to the kids in their private "Tomb of Jesus" bunk rooms. I doubt you'd have to wait more than five minutes before you'd hear the kids praying to God and whimpering for His divine intervention. In fact, talking in tongues is not uncommon among our campers.

Hump: I imagine food and water deprivation, mental and physical abuse, and being enclosed in a one-person cave each night might be the predominant factor.

Rev. B: Oh, ye of little faith! Did not Jesus say: "Suffer the little fat ones to suffer—for verily it is better to look good than to feel good"?

Hump: No, he didn't. Actually the last phrase of that sentence was said by a Billy Crystal character on Saturday Night Live *about twenty years ago.*

Rev. B: Whatever.

Hump: Frankly, Reverend, I think what you're doing is patently deceptive, cruel, brutal, primitive, and barbaric!

Rev. B: Hey, what did you expect? It's a Bible camp!!

96

Is Jesus Worthy of Our Respect?

26 Dec 2010

Ask a Christian precisely which of Jesus' teachings are unique and valid, and what contributions he made to societal conduct or the advancement of civilization that makes his personage worthy of worship and respect, then stand back and marvel at the sound of silence.

Recently I read a comment from a Xtian proposing that even if one doesn't buy into the supernatural deity status of Jesus and dismisses the miracles attributed to him in the New Testament, one must certainly respect and honor the teachings of the man.

My response: *"Really. Such as?"* I asked for ten things that Jesus said that uniquely define him as a great thinker, great teacher, and contributor to societal development or the advancement of civilization. I'd settle for five. I'm still waiting.

I expected that he would eventually come back with "Do unto others as you would have them do unto you." Widely known outside of Christianity as the Rule of Reciprocity, it was professed by Confucianism, Buddhism, the Hindus, the ancient Babylonians, Hebrews, Egyptians, Greeks, et al, well before the Common Era.

Digging deeper, I assumed he'd proffer that Jesus endorsed loving your neighbor as yourself. Yet the same man said he came to instigate discord among family members, turning father against son, mother against daughter, etc. (Luke 12:53). Besides, "love thy neighbor as thyself' was first written in the Hebrew Bible (Leviticus 19:18) fourteen hundred years before Jesus was said to exist. Not a new concept and hardly worthy of awe and admiration. If it were, Xtians would be Jewish and revering Moses as God's chosen one. By the way...by "neighbors" they meant fellow Hebrew neighbors. If you were a Canaanite neighbor to a Hebrew, your love experience may vary...drastically. Jesus' perspective was the same as the Hebrew Bible's. He ministered to the Jewish community

Maybe our Xtian would offer "love your enemy" (Matthew 5). Really? Much as how Jesus loves us all but has no bones about sending freethinkers (his enemy, one supposes) to hell for non-belief, we are to love those enemies who would kill us and who we kill in war? Short of mercy killing, how does loving those you must kill or who want you dead logically reconcile in a rational mind? Since love and death are so closely entwined in the philosophy of Jesus, there should be alarms going off and eyebrows raised...not worship and respect. In fact, the very concept is antithetical to reason or the human condition. Anyone who says they love Osama bin Laden, or Adolph Eichmann, or the guy trying to blow up the plane carrying them and their children is one of two things: a liar or a psychotic.

Perhaps "do not worry about tomorrow...[God will provide]" (Matthew 6) holds some value? Imagine if the whole world did as Jesus admonished and just didn't worry about where their next meal was coming from, or their mortgage payment, or where they will sleep tonight, or how they will pay for their children's higher education. Those aren't prophetic words by which to live. No one besides a welfare-dependent crackwhore or third-world beggar would consider living like that.

The religionist came back with none of these. Instead he said he'd have to do some "research." He also tossed out the ever-popular "you seem to be angry" platitudinous Xtian hand grenade and invoked martyrdom at the hands of my "militant atheism." So much for defending his original contention of Jesus' admirable teachings being worthy of respect...he was now moving onto passive aggressive platitudes and martyrdom.

Virtually everything else Jesus said (and there wasn't an awful lot) related to honoring God, being meek, talking down wealth and productivity, taking abuse, praying to a non-existent being, fixating on sin, and threatening badmouthing you to his dad/self if you don't buy his exalted position.

Only with belief in the supernatural—belief in and fear of what the imaginary afterlife holds—does Jesus have any value. Without that, Jesus is worthy of the same respect and admiration due any one of the thousands of cynic preachers and religious fanatics of his time and eminently less than any of our Founding Fathers, Jonas Salk, or your kid's favorite teacher.

97

Bye, Bye, Black Bird... Hellloooo Jesus!

06 Jan 2011

Over the past week bird and fish kills have been reported in Arkansas, Louisiana, Maryland, Sweden, and Australia, among a few other places. Thousands of black birds falling from the sky, battered and beaten, fish, and crabs washing up on coast lines and river banks have got scientists baffled. But not so the super-religious. The supernaturally befuddled have it all figured out: it's a sign of the End Times. Jesus is coming!

I knew it would come to this. I'd have been disappointed if it hadn't. But when I heard reports of these natural kill events on the news, I had assumed that the usual suspects would be crawling out of their Bentleys and McMansions to proclaim that these are the prophesized early signs, that the End Times were imminent ("...oh, and by the way, send in your twenty-dollar prayer offering and receive your sacred washcloth before it's too late"). I guess they've cried wolf so many times and have said so many ludicrous things that they decided to sit this one out.

Instead, the lead is being taken by amateur fundie prophets of doom who are working themselves into a frenzy quoting biblical verse and offering their thoughtful analysis, explanations, advice, and warnings. These quotes from a blog site are typical of the hysteria.

Justin said: *"This could be a message from god that he is coming back soon. Or it could be the forces of the antichrist in Washington controlling our leaders, which are causing these things as well. The antichrist will give great signs and wonders on the earth and the heaven. Hence UFO's, Dead Birds, Dead Fish, Weird Weather Patterns, Strange earthquakes, etc. The antichrist is here, and will reveal himself shortly..."*

Ed said: *"Fast and pray, fast and pray, then fast some more, then pray and fast and pray. Pray some more, then fast and pray... New world order is thinning out the bird pop so there will be less to feed on them when Jesus commands them to attack."* (http://www.examiner.com/cultural-oddities-in-national/dead-birds-and-fish-bible-prophecy-web-searches-explode)

Certainly these are entirely plausible explanations, if you are Xtian and insane. Meanwhile, verses from Revelation and Zachariah about birds and fish being killed off as a prelude to End Times are being thrown around faster than Hello Kitty underpants at a Justin Bieber concert.

Scientists are still investigating the possible causes and haven't the answers yet. This failure of the experts to provide a snap answer in and of itself is taken as further confirmation by the purveyors of ignorance that Jesus' return is just around the corner. After all, if scientists don't know the cause, the default answer obviously has to be supernatural.

I'm going to be increasing the rates at Eternal Earth-Bound Pets in a few weeks. I'm expecting a big surge in clients for post-Rapture pet rescue. With the May 21 Rapture prediction and all these dead birds and fish adding fuel to the fundie fire, there's money to be made and they won't need it where they're going. Just ask 'em.

98

When Atheist Reason Succumbs to Hysteria We Become Like Them

12 Jan 2011

The mass killings and attempted assassination of Congresswoman Giffords in Tucson, Arizona, last week has created hysteria and knee-jerk reactionary responses from people from whom I would have least expected it. Perhaps my disappointment is my own fault, as I tend to credit freethinkers with using the same reasoned approach to all issues and events as when they rejected supernaturalism. More credit than we apparently deserve.

Over the course of the past few days, I received numerous invitations to join causes and pages on Facebook entitled *"Prosecute Palin for Incitement to Murder"* and *"Remove Palin from Facebook."* Curious, I visited those pages and read some outlandishly speculative comments that were presented as fact—comments so filled with rhetorical hyperbole, so incendiary, and worst of all, so unsubstantiated that had the people positing them been religionists I'd simply have shaken my head and said "Typical."

But these were largely freethinkers, atheists—people who dismiss the supernatural because they demand objective evidence, honor fact (not conjecture), and hold rational thought in high regard, or so I thought. These are some of the actual comments:

"The shooter is a Teabagger!"; "This was all part of a well conceived Right Wing plan!"; "Palin knew this was going to happen!"; "She broke the law and is guilty of conspiracy to murder!"; "We should change the laws for high profile people to hold them accountable for words that kill!"; "She went beyond free speech, like yelling Fire in a crowded theater!"

When questioned as to the foundational evidence for these statements, no substantiations were offered. The pyre was already stacked, the match struck, all they needed was the witch to be delivered to them.

I suggested examination of *Brandenburg vs. Ohio* and *Watts vs. The United States* to better understand the legal criteria for incitement to murder. Palin's gun-themed rhetoric, which appeals to her base and is part of her persona, and the crosshair target imagery do not even vaguely approach that criteria. The critical element being that direct intent to cause harm has to be proven and that mere hyperbole, humor, or offensive methods of stating political opposition are protected under the Constitution. I implored them not to confuse legal accountability with the unethical/insensitive political discourse we all rightly and roundly condemn.

This wasn't received well.

Never mind that my expressed disdain for the far right in general and Palin in particular are well documented.My having oft condemned her hate-filled, unthinking, inflammatory speech as ill-advised and bad for the nation is not enough. My call for rational thinking was largely ignored; worse, it was taken as evidence of my right-wing leanings and proof that I am a Palinist. I was summarily "unfriended" by at least two Facebook "friends."

In the midst of all this, I received this email from an atheist organization in the Southwestern US:

"The WBC [Westboro Baptist Church] *has added another irony as a **right-wing extremist took the lives** [sic] of 6 people wounding 14 more (including Gabby Gifford) will be given hero status by this sick group. If you're in the area please do go to these funerals and help the blockade that will keep the evil of the right-wing out."*

I emailed the group's organizer, commended her efforts to blunt Fred Phelps' despicable plan, and requested her evidence of the shooter's *"right-wing extremist"* credentials. She replied she had no evidence, but it was obvious. I explained that the right is claiming he was a far leftist, also without evidence. When I suggested that her inventive labeling of this maniac—who could as well be far left, independent, anarchist, or simply apolitical but deranged—could damage her and her organization's credibility, she said this:

"I think that [picketing Fred Phelps' demonstration] is a legitimate project for atheists who claim they are also humanists. If my credibility is hurt in the process of getting some action, so be it."

I'll rephrase her comment:

"What harm would it do if I told a good, strong lie for the sake of the cause? A lie out of necessity, a useful lie, a helpful lie…such lies would not be wrong."

If that phrase sounds vaguely familiar to you, kudos. You probably read the chapter in *The Atheist Camel Chronicles* that discusses the Church's endorsement of lying for the faith. Here's the actual quote and its source:

"What harm would it do if a man told a good, strong lie for the sake of the good and for the Christian Church...a lie out of necessity, a useful lie, a helpful lie, such lies would not be against God, he would accept them"—Martin Luther.

The lesson here is that the rationality that permits atheists' rejection of myth doesn't always translate into clear and measured thinking when facing broader real-world applications. Under emotional duress, hysteria displaces reason and the ensuing justification for abandonment of truth and fact reads as despicably as it does from a religionist's pen. Lesson learned.

99

Surrendering the High Ground: The Pitfall of Religious Debate

17 Jan 2011

Religionist: *"Everybody has a chance to go to heaven, if they ask Jesus to forgive their sin."*

Atheist: *"Jesus forgiving your sins means nothing if the person you sinned against doesn't forgive you."*

I witnessed this exchange between religionist and atheist recently. To many of us, it reads as reasonable discourse between two people with opposing perceptions of religion and reality. But that's because we have been raised in a culture where the dominant religion's words of the absurd have become accepted as common parlance. In fact, the atheist has already surrendered the debate high ground by accepting the challenge on the religionist's terms.

In his effort to inject reason to counter a basic proselytizing platitude, the freethinker inadvertently validated the legitimacy of the Xtian's proposal. He did so four times: first, by granting the Xtian's premise of the existence of an imaginary man-god. Second, by imbu-

ing that imaginary being with the ability to grant forgiveness. Third, by allowing the reference to gaining
entry into a fictional place of afterlife to be established
as a valid concern. Finally, by accepting the concept of
"sin" as a meaningful term in secular parlance where
any forgiveness is needed.

Jesus forgiving your sins means every bit as much
to the thinking as Jean Val Jean, Sherlock Holmes, or
Baal forgiving one's sins, so why propose that the fictional god-figure's forgiveness "means nothing _IF_..."? It
means nothing, _period._

That we may use the word "sin" in normal discourse
to mean an ethical lapse is indicative of our evolving
language. But religionists see the word very differently.
Sin is a man-made convention predicated on committing transgressions that violate a supernatural being's
prohibitions or edicts, causing him/her/it displeasure. Thus, since the very concept of sin is fallacious,
it negates any need for forgiveness from anything or
anyone.

Unless this atheist has concerns about entry to paradise after death, or is worried about offending an imaginary supernatural being's sensibilities, or accepts that
not keeping the Sabbath holy is a "sin" necessitating a
spirit's forgiveness (any of which, by the definition of
"atheist," makes no sense), his tack is ill-conceived. The
proper strategy would be to reject the theist's premise,
explain that by virtue of one's reasoned thinking the
proposal is meaningless, and point them to greener
pastures, like Scientologists or Muslims.

When evangelicals propose salvation to an atheist,
they are doing so out of the belief that atheists are simply being stubborn. They have already rejected the fact
of our non-belief, considering it simply a defect that

proselytizing and testimony can repair. That's hardly the time to take their bait.

Twenty-six hundred years ago, Sun Tzu taught that one doesn't intentionally allow their opponent to draw one into battle where the enemy has the terrain that is most advantageous to their strategy. That advise still stands ...no matter how primitive their weapons or weak their minds.

100

A Final Word on Christian Ideals and Values

24 Jan 2011

We've heard time and again that this country was founded on "Christian ideals and values." It's a favored rallying cry of right-wing Christian politicians (or those seeking to placate them,) and their faithful religious supporters. The time to challenge this statement is past due. Let's put a face on this farce once and for all and challenge *them* to provide proof of their contention.

While the first immigrants to this continent were in fact Christian, suggesting that the Pilgrims' (et al) belief system was the "foundation" of what would later become our nation would be like saying that the thirteenth-century invasion of the Mongol hordes into Europe resulted in Poland being founded on "Mongolian ideals." Or that the Scandinavian countries were founded on Viking pagan ideals. The Pilgrims did not welcome other sects or religions. They weren't paragons of tolerance and inclusion. If they existed today, they would likely sail back to England in hopes of re-establishing their repressive society.

Anyone who insists this country is founded on the Ten Commandments hasn't read the Ten Commandments, or hasn't compared them side by side with our Constitution. Which unique to Christianity ideals and values have been codified in our laws that are defined in the Bible? As far as I can discern, none that have stood up to Supreme Court review.

On the other hand, perhaps they will offer burning witches as a Xtian value. Certainly the Bible endorses that, and undoubtedly thousands of early colonists were killed as witches by Xtians. If so, then <u>absolutely</u> that particular Xtian value was embraced in the seventeenth century by the early Xtians of this continent.

Or, if enslavement and genocide of indigenous peoples is a Xtian ideal, then, yes—that too was widely practiced here.

If anti-Semitism and intolerance of other sects and religions is a Xtian value, then indeed that value was honored by early Xtian colonists and continues to this day.

If it's a Xtian ideal to force people to honor their God by imposing blasphemy laws that prescribed fines, imprisonment, or in rare circumstances, death for their violation, then, yes, that particular Xtian ideal was observed here as well.

Xtians may well stake their claim to those ideals and values. They are welcome to them. But nothing in our Constitution speaks to Xtian ideals and values or implies any Xtian dogma, doctrine, or rituals. Freedom of speech is <u>*not*</u> a Xtian value. Nor is freedom of religion, nor the universal right to vote, nor granting private ownership of firearms, nor determining who is qualified to hold office, nor is the abolition of slavery, nor is the concept of equality. Jesus never spoke on these issues, much less endorsed them. And they surely weren't universally practiced in Christian Europe.

This country was a unique and bold experiment. It succeeded largely because it was founded upon rational thought, democratic principles, and our Founding Fathers' explicit intent to avoid the Christian ideals and values that were the very antithesis of rationality and which enslaved Europe for nine hundred years. Those who claim otherwise expose themselves to be undereducated history revisionists, theocrats, fools, or all of the above. This is not a negotiable position to freedom-loving freethinkers.

About the Author

DROMEDARY HUMP is the alter-ego of BART CENTRE, a lifelong freethinker, atheist activist, blogger, and the author of *The Atheist Camel Chronicles: Debate Themes and Arguments for the Non-Believer.* A Vietnam veteran and "atheist in a foxhole," he was awarded the Bronze Star, Combat Infantryman's Badge, and Army Commendation medal. He is a retired senior vice president of a national retail corporation and holds a BA in psychology with a minor in religion.

Mr. Centre is the creator and co-owner of the Eternal Earth-Bound Pets post-Rapture pet rescue website that has received worldwide attention and acclaim. He has appeared on NPR, the BBC, CBC, Australian Radio, the Alan Colmes Radio Show, and many secular and religious radio and television shows across the US and Canada. A full-page article about Mr. Centre and his unique enterprise appeared in *Business Week* magazine (Feb. 11, 2010).

A lifelong New Yorker, Mr. Centre now resides in New Hampshire with his much-put-upon and saintly "quasi-Episcopal" wife of forty-one years and his two dogs. He has two grown, freethinking sons.